I love the spirit I feel when I read what you have written. You deal with a wide variety of topics in a creative and positive way. Outstanding. Your book will be a treasure of thoughts and skill-building techniques that all of us can use. Plus, we learn about the beautiful, 60 year marriage of Bea and Jim.

Britton Wood
Ph.D. LMFT
CFLE Emeritus

My own title for Bea's book would be How to make marriage work—a view from the inside. Bea does explicitly, with detailed examples, what most other people who write about intimate relationships do in a hidden way: develop their approach out of their own relationship struggles. It's heartbreaking to read the dedication: "In memory of Jim Strickland."

Daniel B Wile Ph.D
Diplomate in Clinical Psychology
American Board of Professional Psychology.

Praise for *Fitting Together*

This is an important piece of work for couples. This isn't another expert telling you what to do, this is a wise woman and articulate author writing about the loving and intentional path that she and her beloved husband, Jim, took in creating a humane, enriched relationship that worked for the two of them. It is about the intimacy—emotional, sensual, physical, practical—that they devoted their lives to and that they cultivated in a community of like-minded others. It contains helpful tips and ideas that can be read at any time to encourage couples to come up with their own. The book contains suggestions for deep connection as well as for reconnection at the times that we may feel most disconnected from our partner. It gives a full picture on how to nurture coupledom through pleasant times, joyful times, conflictual times, and, at times, through tragedy. It drips with gems of honesty, vulnerability, and emotional courage. I highly recommend this beautiful read!

Edna Wallace
Marriage and Family Therapist
Licensed Professional Clinical Counselor

Bea's zest for life shines through her lovely book in which, openly and frankly, she illuminates a lifetime of experiences with her husband, and shares her prescriptions for happiness. The choices she makes are authentically existential, quite independent of the judgement of others, and flowing directly from her own heart and mind.

John Price

The words that first come to mind while reading your work are: simple, authentic, and sincere. I love that you are writing from your own experience (certainly a labor of great love). I recognize many of your mannerisms...so I "see" you grinning at times, "herding", and "clapping or clasping your hands together with enthusiasm and delight over a good idea"! Your writing is like

having a personal visit. What you have to say and the way you say it is very important and special to me.
I've gone thru the text and underlined certain parts or phrases that stand out for me personally. A few examples would be "I want to help", "The relationship is an entity. It exists. It's different and separate from you or your partner", "You Could Begin Now", "WE are more important than our tasks" and "For a good time, call your partner". I got a real kick out of that last one!!
I really like your personal stories...how you and Jim met and how very different you found each other to be, the advice that each of your parents gave you, the little skipping in a circle cartoon that reminds you to CELEBRATE!
I like the practical tips such as the need to "water the flowers" because an incredibly good relationship doesn't happen overnight, neglect (great concept) the negative and add to the Love Bank, beware when you embark on stressful undertakings, and to apologize rather than assume your partner didn't notice.
I found the various levels of intimacy interesting i.e. talking about old experiences, current feelings and revealing hopes and dreams for the future.
There's a lot of good content. It's easy reading, inviting and helpful!

Linda Hayes

This is the best book I ever read for couples!! Want connection and communication? Want more sex? You can try out some of the book's fabulous ideas or read aloud to your Sweetie and discuss the possibilities. I've known Bea for 57 years and I saw her relationship with Jim go from loving but stressful to idyllic enjoyment. Fitting Together is the perfect guide to a happy relationship written by a woman who loved, learned and taught it to others.

Marjorie O'Laughlin
Former Treasurer of Indiana
Bea's Friend for 57 Years

"Meaningful Conversation" strikes a cord. We live in an increasingly connected world, yet I think for couples, truly connecting means to disconnect from all other distractions (even for a few brief moments), and commit to giving each other our undivided attention so we can have a meaningful conversation.
The book has a really nice, warm flow, a very personal style which I like a lot. What a very wonderful gift to us for you to share this way! An excellent set of questions that I feel will provide good personal insights and stimulate an engaging discussion.

Muneer Waheed

This is delightful, positive, and informative. I thoroughly enjoyed reading it. I loved the humor. Humor makes the medicine go down, and this will be good, but difficult, medicine for some couples to swallow.

Bob McMain Ph.D.
Professor Emeritus
Department of Social Work Education
California State University, Fresno

"Fitting Together" is fantastic. Full of heartfelt, rich experiences and knowledge for the world to read. It is yet another of your many gifts. Thank you for writing such a gem.

Lida Williams

Great book full of good communication skills. I learned so much more about active listening after reading this. It contains a wellspring of in-depth information about a subject I've mainly associated with couples communication, but I think I need to active listen with everyone.

Cindy Walker

You and Jim have a great story to tell as you really lived what you write about. You both put the Relationship first and then Each counts as well — equalling the "3" in the dynamics: The marriage, the wife, the husband. Most people don't understand this, let alone live it. This is so important. It means accepting, respecting, and honoring what you have already chosen for your life.

Jo-Ann Ash Fairbanks

It's never too late. Focus on growth. Stress the positive. Take time to talk. Fitting Together lays out some of the nuts and bolts for developing a happy relationship. It doesn't happen by accident! Communication, respect, intimacy. . . it's all there. From simple tips to deep sharing of personal experiences, Bea shares insights with both wisdom and humor. Ready to take your relationship to the next level? Here's your road map!

Priscilla Hunt
Executive Director
www.bettermarriages.org

I've enjoyed your writing, Bea, and will share your thoughts and suggestions with couples wanting to move forward in their relationship journeys, crediting you as the source. Thank you for all your contributions benefiting countless relationships through the years, especially ours. Rose and I are reading it together during our morning ritual time, a few pages each day.

Regarding teasing, a friend that used to teach and work in the state prison system said the inmates in his life skills class called teasing "sneaky anger". Thanks for all your work now and over the years Bea. In the short-term I'll use your work as a resource for my October relationship class. Much applause for such a worthy project.

Donnel Lester
in pursuit of the mytho-poetic in men & women

Fitting Together
Connecting Couples in Conversation

Bea Strickland

Fitting Together
Connecting Couples in Conversation

Printing October 29, 2017

Published by
Purple Hills Books
San Jose, California, USA
http://purplehillsbooks.com/

ISBN: 978-0-9863387-6-2

See the author's blog at:
https://BeaStrickland.wordpress.com

In Memory of Jim Strickland
August 18, 1936 – May 26, 2016

I love you
I love you
I love you
I will always love you
I will keep you in my heart forever

CONTENTS

PREFACE

We were married 60 years! Discarding any modesty I will say, we were really happy. We were opposites and had to work out all kinds of differences (for the whole 60 years!) And our marriage was considered a loving, caring model for others! Really! The question they asked was, "What's your secret?"

Our Secret? Since I was asked, I want to tell. I was really happy and I want others to have joy and satisfaction in their relationships. I wrote about some of the things we did to make it such a good relationship and want to share with you in case they are ideas that could work for you two, too.

I want to help. I want to share some of the ideas and actions that my husband, Jim, and I learned to make our 60 year marriage so successful. We were both incredibly happy together because we were intentional about developing a great relationship and did things to make our life together meaningful.

Jim Strickland and I had a marvelous relationship. We loved each other but had very different personalities and needed to learn to fit together. Forty years of Marriage Enrichment through the Association for Couples in Marriage Enrichment, now Better Marriages, kept us working on our relationship while leading other couples in groups and retreats. On the negative side, we still had disagreements, but most of our days were filled with love,affection, and great conversations. We truly *connected*. It was an OK marriage for 20 years but with the last 40 we really had it going well. The secret was learning with Marriage Enrichment and the other couples. We made small changes and adjustments and had lots of sex.

When I taught Parent Effectiveness Training and Couples

Communication classes, a man told me that I could use the internet to keep on helping people after the class ended. I began writing to students: reminders of the skills, a short paragraph, just one screen each week. After a while people urged me to combine these little nudges into a book. I never thought I'd want to but now it makes me happy to write and to think that some of these ideas might contribute to happiness for other couples. It's my "big brag" about our marriage and things for you to try. It keeps our relationship alive to remember and write about the positive things.

I wrote part of the book before Jim died in May of 2016 and some after and didn't change the tense. Some of it says, "We have conversations." Later it's, "We had conversations." I just didn't want to go back and change everything.

Every once in a while I use a little humor that may, or may not, amuse you. You might think it's just a typo; so now you are warned. Maybe it's a joke.

Is this also where I apologize for run-on sentences and poor grammar and not being more talented? I do.

So this book can be read in little snatches if you wish. Hopefully you will have some conversations in the car or at dinner with your loved one about using some of the ideas. Try little pieces of the book in a couples' group.

Look for updates by following my blog:

`https://BeaStrickland.wordpress.com`

We liked Kahlil Gibran's poem, *On Marriage.*
The last verse says,

> Give your hearts, but not into each other's keeping,
> For only the hand of Life can keep your hearts,
> And stand together, yet not too near together:
> For the pillars of the temple stand apart,
> And the oak tree and the cypress grow not in each other's shadow.

Side By Side
Bea Strickland

> The two trees were still standing there.
> We liked those trees and mused on their age
> Had they been standing side by side
> For 60 years as we had?
> We smiled about their faith in waiting thru the winters
> And the hope they had with the new leaves
> We felt connected to them
> By their steady presence.
> Memories of our 60 years
> Comfort me now
> In my heart we're still side by side
> Side by side

Jim and Bea Strickland, 2015

Bea Ambelang and Jim Strickland,
Beloit College, Wisconsin, 1956

Chapter 1

Happy Couple

> Happy couples live longer, laugh more, feel stronger. That's what research says. But that doesn't just *happen*. For the greatest happiness, make it a goal to strive for quality in your closest relationship. Keep your love and all that's good and learn to fit the other pieces together. It's a puzzle, a mystery to play with every day. How can we fit together better?!

Jim Strickland and I grew up within a mile of each other, our parents played bridge together, and we went to the same high school. We were in a play together. I fell in love. We had passion for each other. Then when we were married we found that our personalities were very different: I was emotional, Jim was rational, I was an extrovert, Jim an introvert. He was neat, but for me a spare chair was made to stack stuff. We were opposites in almost any survey. Our priorities were different: I wanted to talk, he wanted to get some work done or watch sports.

We had three little boys and we worked well together during the times of job and financial stress. Then Jim began his 32 year career with IBM and immersed himself in the job. As a traditional stay-at-home mother of the 60s, I continually pleaded for more time with Jim and for him to spend more time with the children. I was an authoritarian mother and the boys rebelled. I was anxious, guilty, insecure, tired and lonely.

When we learned about Parent Effectiveness Training and communication skills, things improved for the children *and* our couple relationship. We listened better, solved problems with less acrimony and more success.

Tragedy struck when our beloved 16 year old son, Jeff, was killed in an automobile accident. We struggled through our grief although neither one of us ever got over it. We could never share the happy memories about Jeff because all we could recall was the pain. We'd start to cry and that was the end of the conversation. It wasn't until 20 years later that I went to a grief group. After that I could reminisce about this wonderful son and enjoy him in memory. We never could talk much to our sons, Jim, Jr or Ken about the loss or help them with their grief. The first thing I did when Jim died was to go to a grief group to get the pain out so that I could relive the happy memories. Of course the sadness still comes by but the joys of our life together will live forever in my heart.

Two years later we made our sixth city move. This time to Nashville, Tennessee. Then, after 20 years of marriage, we found Marriage Enrichment. Ta Da!! It is a program to help couples talk to each other in order to understand one another, solve problems and build a happy life together. That's where we learned how to connect to make our different personalities fit together.

Your Relationship

There are three parts to your marriage. There's you, your partner, and then there's your *relationship*. The relationship is an entity. It exists. It's different and separate from you or your partner.

Your relationship can be seen every day in your interactions as well as in the history of your time together. It is a collection of all your interactions. It's the unique way the two of you harmoniously connect and painfully conflict. A relationship is like a big puzzle. Like a 5000 piece jigsaw puzzle, relationships are so complicated and complex. Just think of all the pieces: two people with their personalities, temperaments, moods, assumptions, expectations, family histories and unwritten rules, problems, worries, fears, needs, habits, aches and pains, unconscious desires, misunderstandings, joys. You need to fit all those pieces together to make the big picture of happy marriage. Those puzzle pieces are not in 2D or even 3D but have a vast number of depths. We make mistakes and hurt each other and apologize–or not, and forgive–or hold our hurts in memory. We make assumptions and judgements, get angry, retaliate, forgive and then come together again.

Usually people ignore their relationship, just taking from it. Your relationship needs to be nurtured. Marriage Enrichment calls this 'being intentional about your marriage'. You learn to do things to help you fit together. As you learn about each other, as you make adjustments and changes, and the picture grows, the relationship grows.

"I will love you forever!" How we wish that were true. But the truth is: You can kill love. People do it all the time. 50% of couples divorce. But 50% of couples do stay together. If you are together, then every day you have the potential for keeping love strong or hurting your relationship. That commitment you made on your wedding day was not just for that day. Your promise is for every day. Your job is to learn to be kind, respectful, loving and to help meet each other's needs. Your partnership is made up of two people who want to be there for each other—for parties on Saturday night or to go to the hospital. So, how do you get started and then keep it going? I have ideas about some of the elements of a great relationship.

Marriage is one of the most important relationships you'll ever have. It's such an important relationship that it makes your whole life happier when it's going well and makes everything more difficult when you are angry with each other. You love (or loved) your spouse more than any other person. You want (or wanted) it to be a lifetime of love. You'd like to fit together in harmony and encourage each other's hopes and dreams. This book is about keeping it that way or remaking it into the best relationship it can be. These are my thoughts about what is essential, important and worth striving for.

Begin Now

Tonight, ask your partner for about 15 minutes of conversation about your relationship.You could try something like, "Hey, can we talk about a question I have? I just want to explore this." Agree that you'll put all teasing and put-downs aside. Ask this question for a positive, warm and loving experience: "What would you like our relationship to look like? A jewel? Like two people, knee to knee, dialoging? Two people hugging? The ultimate friendship? With sex?"

I saw a cute cartoon once that showed a happy couple holding hands and skipping around in a circle and saying, "Oh, yippee, we're both in a good mood at the same time!!" That's a rare occasion and one to be celebrated . . . with lots of kisses and hugs. Life is often difficult and one or both of us gets stressed or tense and may be snappish and cranky. Then we have to endure the worry or distance or loneliness until we can be close, intimate friends again. So, notice the times that you feel happy together and if those times come often, congratulate yourselves. Whenever they come, be aware, talk about how pleasant that is. On the days when it works for you two, acknowledge that you are getting along well and both feeling good. Smile at each other and hug. CELEBRATE!!!

Keep Learning

Just as you water the flowers, take the car in for maintenance, keep your exercise schedule, you should care for your relationship. Learn to have positive conversations, plan time to talk to each other, ask about hopes, dreams, wishes. Read about relationships. Get counseling. Go to a communication skills class, a marriage enrichment group or seminar. We go to a marriage enriching retreat every year—whether we need it or not—because we want our relationship to grow. It turns out that we always need it. No matter what the subject matter is, we always learn something new or are reminded of ways we can be more in tune. Build happy memories that you can keep forever.

Our incredibly good relationship didn't happen overnight. We have false starts, failed attempts and misunderstandings. But sometimes we make little changes and have happy moments that we repeat. The more we're connected to each other, the more alert we are to times when we need to listen to each other's needs or realize that we can play and enjoy life together.

Little gestures may turn things around when you're not feeling as close as you would like, or just add to the joy when all is well. If you accept a party invitation, you don't go there and stand in the corner. You are part of the entertainment. In Marriage Enrichment we say, "Participation is voluntary, but please volunteer to participate." Volunteer to participate in your relationship.

Small changes can have big results. Doing one small thing, like writing a little note to your partner with a compliment, saying "I love you.", doing one of your partner's chores without saying anything, stopping your partner for a hug, may mean a great deal. Even when it seems to go unnoticed, YOU know you did something warm and kind and can feel good about yourself. One of you is moving toward your partner. You don't always know what's noticed and helps maintain the relationship or heal it. But keep doing it.

Positive Actions And Encouraging Words

What have you done for your relationship lately? Your relationship needs care and feeding. Every day. It doesn't have to be a big deal but each day you can honor The Three A's: *affection, affirmation and appreciation*. Affection: hugs and kisses. Affirmation: "I'm so glad you are mine!". Appreciation: "Thank you for cooking with me." "I like watching the game together." All these keep your relationship thriving. Hurtful teasing, those funny derogatory comments, name calling—may not kill you but they can kill a relationship. It's tender and sensitive. Be kind to it. Affection was a big topic at one retreat. One couple said they took frequent hug breaks. We asked when they took those hug breaks. "Oh," they said, "when we climb a flight of stairs, before breakfast, after breakfast, when we meet in the hallway."

Jim and I decided we'd think of more ways and times to be affectionate. Then we thought of the great challenge: could you overdo hugging, kissing and saying, "I love you."? We applied ourselves to mass affection and never did feel like it was too much. I would offer this deal to my communication skills groups, "Call me if you ever feel like you've overdone affection in your relationship."

Research says that couples who idealize each other are happier and stay married. Idealizing and idolizing means to focus on your spouse's good qualities. Often, be romantic and look through the rose colored glasses as you did when you fell in love. If we made a list when we're in a good mood, about all the things we admire about our partner, then we could concentrate on those traits. I don't think we have to lie. Maybe just exaggerate a little.

So remember some of the qualities that you admired and cherished when you first met, how your mate excels, how much you'd miss them, and the kindnesses you receive from your partner. Think of those happy positive things and what you appreciate and enjoy so that you can make your marriage flourish.

Neglect The Negative

So often we find fault and criticize. We tell others about our mate's shortcomings. By discussing the negatives over and over, we rehearse the problems we have and we develop a litany of wrongs. We also invite others to join in with complaints about their partners. There are times when we need to discuss what's wrong but not often. Don't practice finding faults. Don't make finding 'de faults' your position.

There are lots of jokes about marriage, the foibles of men and women. Another reminder of the problems rather than the pleasant aspects of being together. Avoid those comments. Don't feed on the negative. It may not take any more of your energy to think of kind, loving things to say and that's far healthier.

Dr Willard Harley, who wrote *His Needs, Her Needs,* says, "Within each of us is a Love Bank that keeps track of the way each person treats us. Everyone we know has an account and the things they do either deposit or withdraw love units from their accounts. It's your emotions' way of encouraging you to be with those who make you happy. When you associate someone with good feelings, deposits are made into that person's account in your Love Bank. And when the Love Bank reaches a certain level of deposits (the romantic love threshold), the feeling of love is triggered. As long as your Love Bank balance remains above that threshold, you will experience the feeling of love. But when it falls below that threshold, you will lose that feeling. You will like anyone with a balance above zero, but you will only be in love with someone whose balance is above the love threshold"

Focus On Strengths

No one is perfect. We all are a bundle of dysfunction. But we all have goodness and love and generosity, too. I want to think of my partner's strengths and good points more often. I'll start now! That'll surprise him!!

Recently I saw two different sources recommending that couples think and talk about their strengths to encourage good feelings about each other and happiness in the relationship. Why are we strong as a couple? What are we good at? When are we at our best? Test these out as dinner table conversation topics. Also, you could ask your partner, "What are two or three things I could do to make you feel loved?" You get points for asking about ways to say you love your partner. There's always, 'I love you' but also touching, gifts, acts of service, quality time and compliments show your love; we can all use a little more love. Jim and I found that we were feeling very good about each other when we talked about that. We got way off the subject but the idea was to have an entertaining conversation, so it worked!

Apologize

Relationships are so complex and the closer you are, the more potential for friction in simple things. So if you answer your partner in an impatient manner, interrupt, mistakenly tease in a hurtful way, or notice that you are giving commands—then apologize. Don't just assume they didn't notice. "Please forgive me, I want us to feel close, and I goofed."

A good relationship begins with little things, and we all need to correct our course now and then and watch our words and actions with our loved ones.

When we're getting ready for an event, leaving on a trip, or having guests, we get focussed on tasks and then push ourselves and each other. What I would like to do is be alert to those times, take a moment to talk to Jim and affirm that our relationship is the most valued thing and that our goal is to be friends through the chores facing us. Then (perhaps) we're a little more considerate and careful and avoid some harsh moments. It's easy to forget that *we* are more important than our tasks.

If I promised you a million dollars could you be amiable and nice to your partner? Oh, we all could. I just wish I could think of that more often instead of letting small irritations or corrections get in the way of agreement.

My mother and father each (privately) gave me advice when I got married. My mother said, "You have to put up with things when you get married. It's difficult to live with a man so you just have to let a lot of things go." My father said, "Don't put up with things! If there's something you don't like, then speak up about it!" What I've found over the years is that both ideas are good advice. There are times when you should ignore things and times when you should say something and work on it. Knowing which is which is the difficult part.

Dr Willard Harley says[1] "I suggest that you (a) spend time away from children and friends whenever you can and give each other your undivided attention; (b) use the time to meet the emotional needs of affection, conversation, recreational companionship, and sexual fulfillment; and (c) schedule at least fifteen hours together each week. When you were dating, you gave each other this kind of attention and you fell in love. When people have affairs, they also give each other this kind of attention to keep their love for each other alive. Why should courtship and affairs be the only times love is created? Why can't it happen in marriage as well? It can, if you set aside time every week to give each other undivided attention."

1 see his web site www.marriagebuilders.com

Golden Gratitude

In the book, *Authentic Happiness,* Martin Seligman tells us that gratitude is something that is a joy for us to think about and to tell to our partner. We've heard about counting our blessings since we were children and know that's a good way to feel happier. If we count some ways that we're thankful to our partner and then tell them how grateful we are, then we both get to feel happy. It feels good to think about things we're happy about, better to tell our partner and wonderful for them to receive our gratitude. It doesn't have to be big, but put it in an email, on a post-it or couple it with a hug—gratitude is golden.

Our friend, Roy Blom, gave me some of the loving words we could all say more often. "You're so smart", "I love how you notice those things!", "Where would I be without you?", "I appreciate your considerateness and how you handled that situation", "Thank you for remembering to ask me and including me in the decision process."

Stroking each other rather than 'striking' each other. Jim Long says, "The six most important words are, Congratulations, you did a good job!"

Connection and Intimacy

If you already know what a 'connection' with another person is all about, then you probably won't need this explanation. This is my understanding of connection. Connection is a concept, something that happens when you get agreement or understanding from another person. A connection with someone feels good. Agreeability is a personality trait that makes connection happen more easily. It's connecting to go along with someone's statement rather than dispute it. If I say, "What a beautiful day," and you say, "Yes, it is," then we have something in common, we agree with each other and connection happens. All of us can learn to be more agreeable. You make a connection by continuing the direction of a statement rather than contradicting. One person begins a conversation making a bid for connection. Person A makes a statement. Person B agrees. Connection occurs.

But if Person A begins a conversation and Person B disagrees (or contradicts); then that's the end of the conversation or the beginning of an argument. You can connect and agree about something positive or negative. For example, if I say in a positive direction, "Beautiful day today," then your agreement will make a good connection. Something like, "Yes, it is." If we're going together in a negative direction, "It's too hot today," then a connection/agreement would be, "It *is* hot." You're agreeing with the negative statement. If you cannot agree with a person you can still *connect* by active listening or validating their point of view, "You don't like it when the weather is so hot." Disagreements are changing the subject, denying what the other person is saying, arguing, putting them down for what they are saying, and teasing. They are all disconnections. They don't feel good.

Connection means that you are in sync with one another. You focus on each other and listen intently. You show that you care. Connection is kindness, warm interest, attention and awareness going back and forth in conversation. When the connection occurs we enjoy it because we feel cared about and important.

Intimacy develops when you have a good connection with each other. You are on the same wavelength, you understand the meaning of their words, you get it, and you get *them.* First, connection, then understanding and empathy, and then intimacy and love. At the beginning of our marriage we didn't know that connecting, and the intimacy it produced, was valuable or that we could be intentional about making it happen. It took awhile to realize that we could also *prevent disconnection* by agreeing or showing understanding with active listening.

Time together builds closeness and connection. Intimacy is when you feel warm, loving, affectionate and focused on your partner. Connected. It can last just moments or be an evening of closeness. It may be leading to sex or just time when you feel really connected. There are levels of closeness. Talking about facts is not intimate. If you talk about an old experience and feelings you've described before, that's getting closer. When you trust your partner enough to disclose a new happening and current feelings you are saying something more interesting and more intimate. Revealing hopes and dreams and talking about your feelings for your partner gives you the deepest intimacy.

What is a simple pleasure for the two of you in summer? Lying on a blanket out in the backyard after dark looking at stars? Sitting on the front porch holding hands? A picnic in the park? Eating in the backyard? Time in the hot tub? Waiting for the ice cream man? Catching lightning bugs? What little cozy summer treat are you missing? While you're doing that ask what your partner remembers from childhood summers. You are together, focused on each other, with time to talk and listen.

Connection-Disconnection Cycle

It feels good to be close and is worth maintaining with lots of love and attention but every couple has times of good connection and then disconnection. It may be short, neutral disconnection with a lack of focus, a need for alone time or slight distraction. Other times the disconnection lasts an uncomfortably long time and is caused by some hurt, neglect or frustration. It's helpful to understand the connection-disconnection cycle so that you can learn how to maintain rapport or reconnect. To get back to being best friends. We want to be close but we get sick, tired or hungry and our patience wears out. Small irritations that we haven't spoken about pile up and we become generally annoyed at our partner. Then if we haven't been as attentive, respectful or loving, some triggering event can mean a disconnection. A trigger might be an ongoing issue like money, sex, or in-laws. Because we all have unconscious hidden issues we can begin to feel fearful or be hurt and angry. This can break our sensitive connection and cause us to want to fight, stop communicating or feel numb. When you or your partner stop reaching out with a touch or a hug, when you aren't looking at each other, or aren't smiling, that there's some unresolved issue. It takes time to reconnect.

Jim and I talked about the sadness and waste of valuable time in disconnection and agreed that we'd like to get back to being friends as soon as possible. We knew a couple who had argued and then canceled a vacation because they were still distant even after the fight was all over. Jim and I worked it out that *if and when* we became aware that our voices were raised and we felt hot and defensive in disagreement, we would cool off a bit; we'd go off to separate rooms or take a walk by ourselves. One time we argued all the way up to our friend's house, rang the bell and quit fighting the moment the door was opened. An automatic cool-off time. That was a clue that some of our disagreements meant that we needed more attention, more love. Ever afterward we'd give the adrenaline rush some time to dissipate and then try to explain ourselves. One of us would ask, "Do you want to talk?" Then we would take the time to paraphrase what the speaker said. It might sound like, "You were trying to help me and then I was impatient?" The careful responses of *active listening* would slow down our dialogue and keep the argument from re-igniting (usually). Taking a walk together and allowing one person to talk at a time for ten minutes with the other only listening and not being defensive, was effective for us. Sometimes we just never needed to go back to the topic. Later, we'd be very cautious about the reconnection. That meant, "Let's be careful and very polite, wait a bit, then one of us could try a friendly voice and offer a coke or coffee or a walk and see if our partner was ready to connect again." After a late-at-night tiff we'd go to bed and it usually didn't seem to be important to discuss the next morning. What's your experience?

Sometimes the disconnect was more subtle. When one of us seemed extra quiet, didn't respond to a comment or question or gave a curt answer, we'd screw up our courage and ask what was wrong. That's always scary. But if you can retain the ability to think before you react, defend and make excuses, you can avoid escalation to argument. Active listening, which we'll discuss, is part of the answer to reconnection.

It's important to notice your experiences of connection and disconnection and to be aware of how that feels to each of you. Then you know what you want to achieve for your happiest relationship. Happiness is on a spectrum from OK to spectacular depending on your situation. OK means that you can be quietly-best-friends, in separate rooms or different cities. Spectacular can be all the way up to feeling like there's no one else in existence and that this person is part of you. Real is up and down the scale.

I used the diagram of Disconnection-Reconnection on page 16 in my classes. The cute picture on page 17 is what I discovered on my desk after class one evening, and I never found out who drew it. Someone had really connected with the explanation of Disconnection-Reconnection and could cleverly simplify it.

Take Time To Talk

It's important to have time that you spend together, when you don't have distractions of everyday life, when you just focus on each other. Sometimes you find a common interest that gets you all excited; you want to keep talking about it and enjoying the topic and whatever subject it is that you both are concentrating on. You have something to say and are willing to hear each other and time disappears. Listen adoringly just like you did when you were courting. If you value your relationship and want to keep it happy and healthy, plan time to really be with each other. One hour, one day, one weekend of enthusiastic involvement with your partner. A time when you just enjoy each other's company, not discussing problems, just fun together. There's a serious need for playtime and conversation. It gives you something to look forward to and happy memories. The dessert of life. For a good time, call your partner.

Disconnection - Reconnection Cycle

Triggering Event

- Money
- Sex
- In-laws
- Children
- Lateness
- Sarcasm
- Teasing

Filters

- Negative interpretation
- Judgement
- Labeling
- Beliefs
- Expectations
- Lack of tolerance
- Emotional states

Hidden Issues

- Rejection
- Helplessness
- Fear of failure
- Power

Preventive Maintenance

- Emotional support
- Adequate rest
- Healthful nutrition
- Communication skills
- Affection

Relationship Repair

- Showing Understanding
- Expression skill
- Time out
- Problem solving
- Apology

Disconnection - Reconnection Cycle

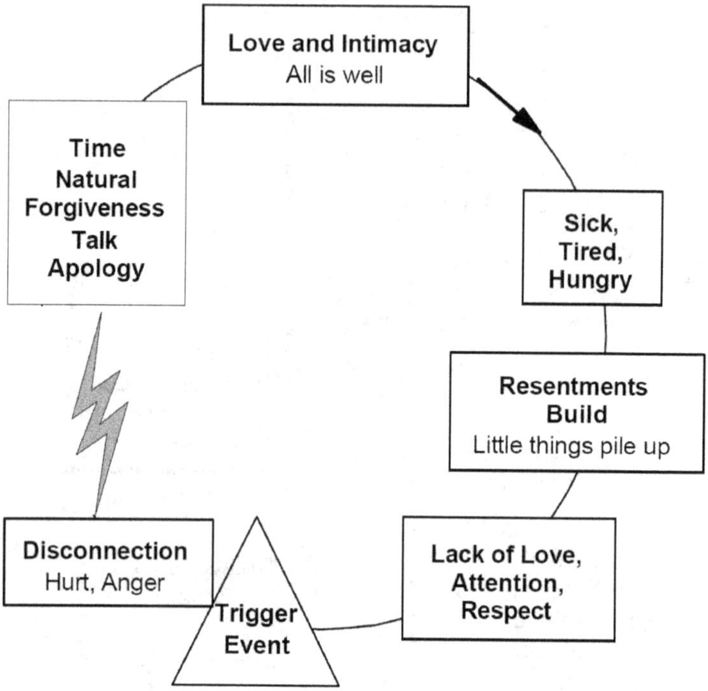

Disconnection - Reconnection Drawing

Please Listen
Anonymous

When I ask you to listen to me,
and you start giving me advice,
you have not done what I have asked.
When I ask you to listen to me
and you begin to tell me why I shouldn't feel that way,
you are trampling on my feelings.
When I ask you to listen to me
and you feel you have to solve my problems,
you have failed me (strange as that may seem).

Listen—all I asked was that you listen—not talk or do,
just hear me
I can "do" for myself
I am not helpless—maybe discouraged and faltering—
but not helpless
When you do something for me that I can and need to do for
myself, you contribute to my fear and weakness.

When you accept as a simple fact that I feel what I feel,
no matter how irrational
then I quit trying to convince you
and get down to the business of understanding
what is behind the irrational feeling
and when that is clear, the answers are obvious
and I don't need advice
Irrational feelings make sense,
when we understand what's behind them.
so please listen and just hear me
and if you want to talk, wait a minute for your turn
and I will listen to you.

Chapter 2

Active Listening

What? Why? Who? How? When? Benefits?

> "I know that you believe you understand what you think I said, but I'm not sure that you realize that what you heard was not what I meant." Robert McCloskey

Active listening is the way to let others know you understand the meaning of their words when they are telling a problem, are emotional, or saying something important.

I taught active listening for 37 years in Parent Effectiveness Training and Couple Communication, but I know that some people never quite understood the idea of *active listening*. Some were nervous about using it and never worked at it, and some forgot all about it. This is an attempt to explain it thoroughly and sell it wildly as the great cure for many problems. It works so well for me—giving or getting. This is the advice I want to give everyone who wants to be helpful and a good listener. To listen to someone is to give love. It gives a feeling of connection and bonding to speaker and listener whether for a short conversation or a life-long marriage.

Before describing active listening, let me say that there is nothing wrong with sympathy—which sounds like, "I'm so sorry" or questions like "What happened?" but active listening is better.

Passive Listening, being silent and attentive is also helpful, but active listening is more empathic.

When someone active listens to my problem it is the ultimate healing response. It lets me hear what I am saying and then I can decide if I've expressed it well and if I really mean what I've conveyed. I often solve my own problem when someone uses active listening and that feels victorious; unlike the frustrating feeling when I get advice that I don't want.

What is active listening? Active listening is responding to what you hear someone say. You demonstrate your understanding by paraphrasing the person's message. You say a short phrase in your own words about the other's feelings or the meaning of what they said. It's checking out whether you've heard correctly, and if that's what they meant to say. Active listening demonstrates your understanding and empathy. Active listening is a compassionate response.

It's also called empathic listening, reflective listening, showing understanding, compassionate response; it's feedback to show that you realize the essence of the message. When your partner has a problem, is emotional, or has something important to say, you owe it to them to listen. You want to listen; you believe you're listening. And somehow you need to convey that intent. When you active listen you are respecting your partner's ability to resolve their own issues. Active listening might sound like "You're having a really hard time." Or "I guess you feel worried." Or "That's so scary."

Active Listening Basics

To emphasize the basic ideas of active listening:

- Listening when your partner has a problem, is emotional, or has something important to say.
- Responding with empathy. Empathy is the ability to understand another person's feelings.
- Acknowledging the other's feelings, problem or ideas.
- Reflective listening, showing understanding, or repeating in your words the essence of the message.
- Acceptance that feelings are always legitimate; they are neither right nor wrong.
- Being sensitive to another person's feelings and letting them know you are sensitive and are not denying their feelings.
- Noticing the attitudes and feelings involved in the message given.
- Telling the person as exactly as you can what you heard them say, in terms of the attitudes and feelings you heard expressed, in as few words as possible.

How Do You Active Listen?

- Get yourself and your advice and ideas out of the way.
- Do not respond with your own thoughts or analyze what they said.
- No judgement or evaluating, sympathizing, giving opinions, using logic or persuasion, analyzing, advising, ordering, or questioning.
- Ask yourself, "What is s/he feeling?"
- Respond with:
  "You feel ________________";
  "You feel ________________ about ________________"; or
  "It sounds like you feel ________________."
- Often you'll be tentative with your response and will end with a questioning tone.
- Don't ask: Who, What, When, Why, or How —questions. Responding to questions moves your brain to thinking and away from feelings. We hope to help a person think about solving a problem but that happens naturally after most of the feelings are expressed. With active listening you stay out of their way and let them process the feelings and then move to thinking by themselves.
- Do not add or subtract from the sender's message.
- Deal with the feelings you hear instead of staying with the facts.
- It's OK to repeat the feeling word your partner used.
- Or you can use words different from the sender without changing the meaning.

Body Language

Listening isn't just an ear task. Our eyes, our body, our comments confirm our attention. When we use silence, eye contact, head nods, some verbal acknowledgment to let our partner see and hear our understanding, we make a qualitative difference in their feeling of being heard. Orienting your body toward the speaker, uncrossing your arms, leaning forward also indicate interest.

Eye contact means gazing at the person's eyes, maybe just one eye. The term "Soft Eyes" is used to express the combination of facial muscles used to look caring but not condescending, interested but not suspicious, intent but not fixed, open but not too wide or vacant. Occasionally move your eyes to different parts of the face or briefly glance away.

Then—no fixing, no advice, unless they ask, and even then advice may not be wanted. Make sure they want your ideas and then just give suggestions. Maybe, "That's really rough." or "Do you want to say more." Adding a warm, soft, sympathetic voice helps your words sound earnest and sincere.

Ways To Describe Active Listening

- Restating the other person's message in your own words.
- Paraphrasing.
- Demonstrating that you understand what has been said.
- Reflecting feelings.
- Listening for the feelings underlying the words. (The feelings may be spoken or unspoken.)
- Summarizing, clarifying, checking out.
- Guessing at the meaning of your partner's words.
- Expressing understanding of another person's feelings, problem or idea.
- Connecting instead of correcting.

Feelings

I'm using the words 'emotion' and 'feelings' interchangeably. Consult Google for differences.

We all have feelings. At least 120 a day. Fleeting or lasting awhile. Pleasant or painful. A child's book described feelings as Sad, Glad, Mad and Scared. Then there are all the variations of those emotions.

Sad: dejected, depressed, disappointed, embarrassed, hopeless, ignored, insecure, lonely, misunderstood, overwhelmed,sorry, unappreciated, used, useless, weepy

Mad: angry, annoyed, cranky, fierce, frustrated, furious, grouchy, hostile, impatient, irritated, judged, manipulated

Glad: accepted, appreciated, brave, calm, confident, content, creative, eager, excited, exhilarated, generous, grateful, happy, hopeful, involved, loving, optimistic, peaceful, pleased, proud

Scared: afraid, alarmed, anxious, concerned, fearful, frightened, persecuted, pessimistic, pressured, rejected, startled, terrified, threatened, wary, worried

Feelings often begin with a situation which starts a reaction. First, I see what I interpret as danger. My brain signals adrenaline to energize me to action. Then I have thoughts and feelings. For example: I'm on my way to teach a class and driving 65 miles an hour behind a big van. I see the tail lights go on and he's stopping! I brake quickly. A small crisis. As this occurs I have many thoughts of the past, present and future. "What's happening? Oh, gosh, I'm glad I was paying attention. Will that car behind me be able to stop? Why are the cars on either side still moving? Will I make it to my class on time?"

Along with the adrenaline and thoughts, come feelings in my body; my breathing and heart beat change to give me the energy for a flight or fight response. I describe this excitement as 'a mix of emotions': fear, relief, irritation, puzzlement, curiosity. Mixed feelings—like the old joke about your mother-in-law going over the cliff in your new Cadillac.

Feelings can be mild, medium or strong. They can be immediate or delayed. Feelings signal excitement or a problem. Present feelings are compounded by old unresolved experiences and problems.

Strong feelings take awhile to go away. The adrenaline circulates in your system and takes some time to dissipate.

Feelings can also begin with random thoughts.

Anger is an emotion, but usually a second emotion, coming after fear or frustration.

If someone is listening and names the feelings it adds validity to the emotion. It helps normalize. Makes it OK to have the feeling. And it's OK to have any feeling as long as we don't act on the feeling and hurt others or ourselves. I had a sign once that said,"I can have any feeling I want." Acknowledging the feelings makes them sound less fearsome. Like fog in the sunshine they begin to evaporate.

When you become more conscious of your feelings you can become objective and begin to relax and think about what you want to do or change. Or you just feel relieved and go on to other things.

Sample Sentence Starts

The idea with active listening is that you demonstrate in your own language that you have understood the problem and/or feelings of the other person. See possibilities below:
You feel ________________ about ________________
You feel ________________
I guess you feel ________________
You appear to be feeling ________________
I somehow sense that you are feeling ________________
Let me see if I understand; you feel ________________
Let's see if I'm with you; you feel ________________
Perhaps you're feeling ________________
What you're saying is that ________________
I hear you saying ________________
I really hear you saying ________________
It sounds like ________________
You really ________________
It's so ________________
That's so ________________
It seems like ________________
It makes you wonder if ________________
You wish ________________
You want ________________
You'd like ________________
You think ________________
You mean ________________
Could it be that ________________
I wonder if ________________
I'm not sure I'm with you, but ________________
Correct me if I'm wrong but ________________
It appears that you ________________

You could write a bunch of active listening responses to have ready for all occasions:
Supply some real sincerity, intensity and feeling in your voice along with eye contact.
"That really made you mad." "You feel let down." "It hurts your feelings." "How sad you feel."
"You were delighted." "That was very scary."

The Good Listener

The newpaper headline said, "The Good Listener" and I got excited, "Oh, they're going to talk about active listening!" Wishful thinking. But this is what I wish they'd said:

> Active listening, or reflective listening, is just trying to understand your partner by feeding back a few of their thoughts when they have a problem, are emotional, or saying something important to them.

Active listening is not fixing problems. It's doing less. Which is so much more welcome. Think of your partner wanting to say, "I don't want you to fix it, I don't want suggestions, I want to hear that you heard me. It's such a relief to have someone understand."
Usually all we want when we are stressed, upset, or have a problem, is for someone to demonstrate that they heard. Our need is, "Did you get that?" "Do you hear that I'm hurting?"

Active Listening Because:

- Keeps the ownership of the problem with the person involved.
- Frees the other of troublesome feelings so that s/he can solve their problem.
- People become less afraid of negative feelings.
- Promotes a feeling of understanding between and among people.
- Facilitates problem solving.
- Lets the person hear that you get what they are saying and they don't have to repeat.

The Listening Mindset

"Seek first to understand", Stephen Covey tells us in his book, *The Seven Habits of Highly Effective People.*

Active listening is the way to let others know we understand that we get it when they are telling us a problem or are emotional. But it's more than a tool for helping others; it's a different mindset. Active listening is the effort and attempt to really hear others, pay attention in a different way and to connect. It's like saying, "I want to be with you and understand while you explore your feelings."

Active listeners keep away from judging, labeling and interpretation. Listeners think "What is this person trying to convey? What does he mean?" rather than dismissing someone's words as stupid, silly, or meaningless and "I know better than they do what they need." "Seek first to understand."

Arguments

We argue when we don't feel heard. We all want to be understood. If you're not listening when I'm being vulnerable, I first feel frustrated, then hurt and then angry. I'd better talk louder. I can kind of hear what you're saying but I didn't get a chance to say all that I wanted to, so I'll just keep yelling. Oh, now I'm even madder, I can hear you yelling about something completely wrong and that just frosts me. What??!! You still didn't get it. You idiot. I think I'll just stomp out of here. Then you'll get the point.

Instead Of Arguments

Listening! That can be the answer. Any time you have heated talks, when one of you raises your voice, even just a little, it's time to slow the conversation down and time to listen to the other's point of view.

It doesn't matter that it's a trivial thing you're talking about. It doesn't matter that you're *right*.

When you realize that your discussion is escalating—breathe deeply, change directions, let the thinking part of your brain take over and be the one to *listen*.

Who will be the one to say, "Let me really listen to you. Please tell me again. What is it you need?" Then demonstrate that you understand by paraphrasing your partner's main idea. Then ask if they want to say more before you tell them your side of things.

Listening! The relationship gift. A gift of your time and attention.

When you listen to your partner and say, "I understand, *but* . . ." you are not really active listening. It's like saying, "But I know how to fix this better than you do. Let's get it over with. I hear you but I don't care. I'm not really on your side. I'm really only interested in what I want. "

Active listening is a gift of accepting and loving. There are no strings attached. When you really listen you show that you hear and understand with no 'butting' in. No fixing and advice. You listen and paraphrase with no agenda of your own. Pure active listening is soothing, comforting, relieving, healing and satisfying. It allows someone to talk out problems, maybe solve them or just air them out. It sounds like,
"You feel angry about that."

"You're having a really hard time."
"That isn't working for you."
"You're so worried."
"It just seems too complicated."

Or active listen during happy times to understand and acknowledge the joy. When your partner shares good news and you respond with active listening you are practicing what researchers call 'Capitalization'. Capitalize and accentuate the success with congratulations. You celebrate their happiness and both of you get positive feelings:
"I guess you must be thrilled."
"It feels like a great success."
"You're so happy about it!" Build your communication skills for a safe way to talk about sensitive and important things. It's worth taking time to learn ways of complaining and stating problems in a neutral, non threatening way. We're all tender beings underneath. We need connection for our sorrow and joy.

One technique Jim and I worked out was to stop when we begin to get angry and raise our voices. We call a time-out, and then go for a walk with the idea that one person will get to talk awhile with only active listening as a response. No defense. After ten minutes or a whole day in between, the other will be the talker. This takes the heat out of the disagreement. We guess that being outside in nature brings a bigger perspective and walking may be soothing or help us think. Walking increases deep breathing which is nourishing to the brain. Then, too, we're out in public and may unconsciously be more careful about how we say things. Sometimes we'll see where a misunderstanding has occurred; sometimes the listening will solve the problem; other times we'll spot a conflict that we both need to mull over for a day or two.

Another factor in taking a walk together is that our eyes move around, viewing the changing scenery, as we're walking along.

Linda Hayes just coupled the concept of eye movement therapy with the idea of taking a walk to talk about something emotional.

Linda said, "One of my friends is a Family Life Counselor. This past week EMDR (Eye Movement Desensitization and Reprocessing) came up in the conversation and she explained that it is a technique used to help trauma victims. As the eyes move back and forth, the process helps a person see disturbing material in a new and less distressing way. I think that's a reasonable explanation. I'm mentioning it because you and I have had this conversation about the benefit of eye movement when taking walks. I liked hearing the technical explanation."

Maybe walking and talking can be a natural way of EMDR. You don't realize it, but you're getting extra therapy when you walk, talk and glance around at your surroundings.

Why It Works

Differences of opinion are less irritating if each can tell their point of view and be acknowledged. I don't need to have my way, I need to be understood and have Jim demonstrate understanding with active listening and compassion.

When couples talk about an issue and one talks and the other empathizes with active listening, the urgency, pain and heat are taken out of the problem. There's such relief in having your partner understand you, it's calming. Active listening demonstrates that they care, that you and your needs are important. It shows respect of feelings which translates to respect of the other person. It says, "Your feelings are important to me, you are important."

When someone active listens, sometimes a solution immediately presents itself. Sometimes taking time away from the problem will let you come up with an idea of how you can work things out to mutual satisfaction. Other problems may require brainstorming to find the ideal answer to each of your needs. This kind of respectful listening to each other's perspective builds and maintains a strong, happy relationship.

One book that is designed for a couple to learn ways to communicate and solve problems successfully, is *12 Hours to a Great Marriage* by Howard Markman and Scott Stanley. They talk about the filters that come from our backgrounds and experience—the beliefs, emotions and interpretations that distort our communication. What we mean to say and what is heard may be very different. Deliberately slowing down your interaction with active listening will ensure that you understand what your your partner is trying to say and allow for correction. "I know you believe you understand what I said but I am not sure you realize that what you heard was not what I meant!"

Shorten Problem Time

Another reason for active listening! Saving time. If I have a problem or am emotional and Jim attempts to reflect or paraphrase what I've said, then I don't have to go on and on, repeating, explaining or trying to convince him that I'm hurting. He proves that he understands and I can have that relief of knowing that someone else realizes how I'm suffering. I'm pretty much done. He gets it; he shows he's aware of the essence or meaning of my words. It shortens the listening time and the sad time and we can both feel better.

Bea: "I'm so scared!!" Jim: "You're really worried." Bea: "YES!!" Followed by big sigh and hugs.

Be On His Side

Jim told me about a disappointment he'd had with someone over something and only later did I realize that I hadn't listened to him. I had defended the other person rather than hearing Jim's irritation and frustration. He initiated a conversation, was trying to tell me something, and I took us in another direction. That's one of the things that others have done to me, too. When it happens I experience double frustration and wish I'd never said anything at all.

I wish I had said something to Jim like, "He really let you down. Or, How infuriating. Or, You're worried that it will ruin things."

It's one of those things to watch out for and one more example of the need for active listening—your loved one's thoughts and feelings are what is important.

Fidgeting

I didn't know I fidgeted when I listened to people. Then I started noticing because I read about it in a book and there I was. Twiddling a ring, scratching, moving my tongue over my teeth (a lot) after lunch. (I didn't realize that it showed.)

Of course we don't have to be listening intently to every word another is saying. Sometimes we are casual talkers and relaxed listeners.

When we do want to pay a lot of attention to someone who is telling their feelings, talking about a problem or something very important to them, then we want to keep our wiggling and jiggling to a minimum. You wouldn't want to look completely still either. Instead, we'll be changing expression, nodding, using good eye contact without staring.

The idea is to convey that this is very important to us to hear every word and take it seriously. At a John Gray seminar, one exercise was to listen to a person without speaking and look like this was the most important thing you ever heard. It was so satisfying to tell a story and have it received like that. The intentional focus felt so good.

Patience To Listen

I was reading Pat Love's book, *The Truth About Love*, and she was asking: "Can you listen without interrupting? Can you continue to hear when you disagree? Can you be patient enough to hear it all? Can you sit quietly as your partner explains his/her position?" Oh, these are hard things to do! Don't you just want to jump in and correct or object? Isn't it amazing how fast you can forget to be a listener and interrupt with your own story or protect your viewpoint or belief? I think we should discuss how easy it is to get in an argument by not listening. Our goal is to create a safe environment to talk about difficult subjects. I think I need frequent reminders.

From Feelings To Thoughts

When someone listens to me it helps me think about my words and consider whether I truly believe what I said. I increase my awareness about triggers and hotspots. I can calm down or decide that I have a problem to solve.

Just because I know something intellectually doesn't mean I am fearless or that I don't get angry. I must pay my taxes, I do understand that; but I may still get fearful, angry and agitated. My thoughts get it, but my feelings are aroused.

This is the situation that active listening was made for! I don't need anyone to tell me the facts or try to talk me out of my feelings. I need someone to understand and acknowledge my feelings. Sure they're irrational. But natural.

There are lots of responses that show understanding and acceptance of those feelings while not agreeing that they are truth: "How painful." "Scary!" "So irritating, isn't it?"

When my feelings are reflected I feel validated, normal and calmed. I can think again instead of being stuck in emotion. When I'm calm I can accept the things I can't change and begin to think rationally again.

Listeners

Most people who practice active listening, (empathic listening, reflective listening, showing understanding) find that problems are solved faster, misunderstandings are eliminated and the speaker gains relief and is grateful to the listener. Oh, how we love being understood. As a listener you may find that it gives you joy to show your caring by active listening. It could even feel like a superpower to be a good listener.

Just Begin

Everything is difficult to begin with. There are some who are wary of attempting to active listen—maybe fearful of doing it wrong, being laughed at, sounding artificial or condescending. No skill is ever easy at the beginning, there are always mistakes while you're mastering a skill. It's difficult to understand what people mean, but when you work through the awkward moments you have a powerful helping technique to give your loved ones. Start with little sounds if you are hesitant—"oh, ahh, awww, ugh, uh oh, umm." Have a serious and concerned facial expression. Turn toward the other, lean in a bit. Focus, concentrate. Tell your partner that you want to listen better, that this is new to you.

Guess at the feelings expressed: "You're worried?" "That was so frustrating!" Or repeat a few of the words you heard: "You didn't know what was best." "It was so hard to figure out." Your partner will be delighted that you want to listen well. Ask for patience while you learn to do this. Be patient with yourself as well. It's not always easy to pick out the right words or meaning to feed back. Maybe you'd feel best trying it out at first with frustrated strangers—like in a busy supermarket checkout lane.

A Gift

Active listening is a gift. When someone has a problem and/or emotion, give them the gift of demonstrating that you understand—show that you really hear them. It's a gift of your time. It is a technique, a skill, but the intent is empathy. You're not doing it *to* them, you're doing it *for* them. Active listening says, "You are important to me, I accept your feelings, nothing you say is trivial." It's a real service. It's kindness and compassion in action.

When you have a few successes it's very reinforcing for you both to know that it makes a difference.

Relationship is Important

Because your relationship is so important you can learn to listen better. You can help your partner feel the delight of being understood and accepted. Pretend you're going to get a million dollars worth of love if you can make your partner believe that you are treasuring every word they say!

CHAPTER 3

I-MESSAGES

If you do these things *perfectly* you will be happy together forever:

- Make your relationship a top priority
- Give affection, affirmation, attention
- Never insult by sarcasm or name-calling or making fun of your partner
- Listen without interrupting, criticizing or correcting. Acknowledge and active listen.
- Express gratitude for your partner
- Do favors, use your manners, be of service, give gifts
- Spend lots of time, especially quality time together, with meaningful activities, conversations and fun
- Agree more often than disagreeing.

Of course, it's impossible to be *perfect* so the next best thing is to control conflict with I-messages and problem solving.

Aristotle said, "To be angry is easy but to be angry with the right person at the right time, in the right way for the right reason, for the right purpose, is not easy."

Why Use An I-Message

Good relationships are a key to happiness. When you're happy together you have peace and joy but every couple has problems. When there's conflict with your loved one you are both troubled. It's very important to know how to resolve disputes. I-messages are the beginning of creative conflict resolution.

Conflict comes from many directions: having different desires or values or goals, your unmet needs, misunderstanding your partner's words or actions, teasing, put-downs, inattention, lack of affection, corrections, criticisms and wanting to be right. These things are exacerbated by being sick, tired or hungry. Acoholics Anonymous advises one to *halt* and watch out for hunger, anger, loneliness and tiredness.

There will be conflict in your relationship. The more time you spend together and the closer you get, the more friction is possible. You rub each other the wrong way. Little things begin to be annoying. Their "stuff" is your mess. Lateness begins to feel disrespectful. You have differences about money. There are too many in-laws and not enough sex. Then there are the hidden issues like the fears of being rejected, betrayed, abandoned, not being loved or extra sensitivity to criticism, correction. It's so easy to blame or lash out, get angry, insult and name-call. What follows are hurt feelings, defensiveness and arguments. This builds a pattern of hurtful encounters which crowd out the loving time together. It begins a cycle of grudge collection and retaliation along with the disconnection.

Criticism vs. Complaint

There's a difference between criticism and complaints. Criticism and correction cause defensiveness, not the way to a happy relationship. We're all tender and easily hurt, though we work hard at hiding our vulnerability. It's OK to state our wants and to let our partner know about problems. I-messages are the answer to complaining effectively so that your partner can listen with the least possibility of being hurt or angry. When you become aware of a problem you can choose to state your needs rather than blame or criticize. You can reach higher to avoid hostility and use language that helps solve problems and not escalate them.

Soft Start

John Gottman suggests that when you have a disagreement with your partner that you begin your confrontation gently—a soft start. "It's not what you say but the way that you say it."

I-messages provide the soft start—the best way to tell about a problem with the lowest risk of hurting feelings or escalating a conflict.

Forming an I-Message

The idea of an I-message is to describe what you see and hear, your feelings, and the consequences to you. An I-message contains facts, your feelings, and the effects of the actions.

An I-message is the best way to tell others that you have a problem with their behavior. It is a sentence that consists of what you see or hear your partner doing, their unwanted actions, how you feel about that and what the consequences are for you. It is the effect on you, not threats or how you'll punish them. No blame. You are describing your problem and not interpreting their actions.

What is the format for an I-message? The complete I-message consists of three parts— my feelings, the behavior, the effect on me—in any order, and as short as possible; no one likes a long recitation of their sins.

I feel _______ when you _______ because _______

Or When you _______ I feel _______ because _______

The I-message sometimes consists of only one or two parts but is not as effective as a three part I-message:

One part - "I feel _______"

Two parts - "I feel _______ when you _______" or "When you_______ then _______."

What Are Feelings?

- 'Emotions' and 'Feelings' are words that can be interchanged.
- Sad, Glad, Mad, or Scared are feelings (and the many variations: unhappy, pleased, angry, worried)
- Feelings come from thoughts, although they may be so rapid that we think they precede thoughts
- As we have experiences and take in information that we see or hear, then we think about that. We take information from our senses as "facts". We like or dislike those facts. We translate the facts to feelings.
- We're conscious of some emotions, other emotions are unconscious
- We notice the effects of feelings in our bodies (tense shoulders, sweaty palms, clenched jaw, stomach ache)
- Feelings come and go, can be mild or strong or mixed, fleeting or obsessive.
- Basically, feelings are pleasure or pain, they can be intense or mild, and we have hundreds every day.
- Strong emotions generate adrenalin and take a while to disappear even after the problem seems understood and resolved.
- Anger is a second emotion which means that before we get angry we are hurt, embarrassed, frustrated, or scared.

What's Behavior?

- Describe the behavior (actions, what the person is doing or not doing.)
- Describe only what you see or hear (no judging and blame words like sloppy, rude, thoughtless, reckless—"them's fighting words" and will inflame any discussion)

Consequences: the effect on me

- What happens to me as a result of your behavior or of my feelings.
- Often I need to spend extra time, money or energy to correct a situation.
- The effect should be as concrete and tangible as possible.
- No punishment to the other person or threats.

When to use them

- When I have a problem
- When I'm not getting my needs met.
- When the other person's behavior is interfering with my needs.

They will help me to

- get what I want
- begin a discussion about a problem
- solve my problem
- not hurt anyone's feelings
- not blame anyone
- help the other to want to change behavior.
- keep our relationship strong
- not pretend and resent
- not get aggressive or blowup
- avoid judging, threatening, blaming or ordering
- take responsibility and own my problem
- be assertive.
- initiate problem solving

Examples Of I-Messages

(Feel free to borrow and use these.)

- When you leave the wet towel on the bed, it irritates me because it makes the sheets damp.
- I worry when you are late.
- I get scared when you go 80 miles an hour.
- When you don't call to say you'll be late, dinner gets cold and stale and that's frustrating.
- It hurts when you tease me about my cooking.
- If you leave the plate with egg on it, it's hard to get off and that irritates me.
- When you say 5 minutes and it's more like 15, I get annoyed having to wait.
- If I agree to go on one errand and you add more places to stop, it's frustrating because I have other plans for my time.
- When you don't come home til 8 the children have to go to bed and there's no time for quality family time and I'm disappointed and so are the kids.
- I get scared when you make an unexpected purchase, because we'll be short on money for our bills.
- When you drive so close to the car in front it takes away the enjoyment of our trip because I'm so tense and scared.

Subtleties Of I-Messages

Maybe you'll find it easy to formulate an I-message. For me it was a new way of speaking and required some thought. I practiced by writing a great many on paper before sending them, so I could see if they were free of insults. Being extra careful worked so well that I took for granted that I could manage I-messages, then relaxed, became more casual and would get into difficulty. Even when I sent what I thought were perfect I-messages I would have problems occasionally. Even with the best motives it could be heard as an attack. Sometimes people cooperate right away. Other times a simple I-message can become a problem to the other person. If a person objects after your I-message, the best way to deal with defensiveness is to *active listen.*

As in doing anything new, I needed lots of practice. I had better results with people who were not family. I had a job as Youth Coordinator at the Methodist Church and using I-messages with the youth group was like magic. I had more difficulty at home. Some people in my classes in Parent Effectiveness Training found the opposite to be true—easy at home, harder at work or with a friend. You don't want to send I-messages too often but you do need to practice your skill. We were glad we led Marriage Enrichment groups because we could solve problems there while on our best behavior.

Donnel Lester suggested:

Eliminate the word "you" as much as possible to avoid triggering the recipient taking the comment personally. For example, "when the car gas tank is left empty and I'm delayed by needing to add gas, it can make me late for an appointment" or "when grocery supplies are used up and not added to the grocery list, I may not be able to fix a proper dinner when I need to." It isn't always possible to eliminate "you" but it softens the message when it is possible. One can always enhance it after the first attempt with something like "I'm appealing to you for your help here" if the first attempt falls on deaf ears.

Variations

Sometimes a preface to the I-message may be necessary to establish that you want to tell your partner something that's bothering you and ask if this is a good time. "Would it be OK to talk about something now?" Or "I need to tell you something, is that OK now?" "I need to say something, is this a good time?" This is an alert and a caution for your partner to be ready to listen more thoughtfully.

Some communication skills programs suggest that you begin with a compliment or telling what works well. Beginning with a positive comment does two things: it gives you a moment to be aware that there are good things happening in your relationship and for your partner to hear that. This adds to the soft start if you both agree that this is a useful tool and not meant as manipulation. Openness means we discuss the best ways to approach issues and not a way of tricking each other.

Sometimes along with the I-message you can also tell the person what you want or wish they would do.

You can ask for active listening at the same time. "Please tell me what you hear me say so that I know I've said it the way I meant to." Formal? Stilted? Not natural? Yes, but better than a fight. And we know that many communications are unnatural but necessary for harmony—like using manners. You might rather use your fingers but you use a fork. Most of us do, although I had a student whose wife sent him because he was a bad example to the kids when he enjoyed eating salad with his fingers.

Don't fix blame, fix problems. I-messages often effect a change and solve a problem. If the other person's needs are important to them and they can't change their behavior you can go on to Problem Solving, finding options to meet both your needs.

Slow Thought Process

There are times when we freeze and don't explain ourselves and offend by not responding. Jim said, "Let's cook together and have a special dinner tonight." I thought that was a good idea, knew I should be enthusiastic, didn't want to because I was tired and had planned to make something quick and easy and go to bed early with a book, then I felt guilty, resented having to reconsider, wished he'd said something earlier, so I didn't say *anything at all*. Then I suppose my brain got stuck, just couldn't figure out what to say. I didn't correct the impression I had given; I just blanked it all out. The next day we finally talked about it and I learned that Jim had taken the silence as a rejection, felt hurt, then angry. At least we brought things up to discuss and clear up later. Each time we discussed a problem later, and were careful to keep *that* from becoming an argument, we added to our understanding of each other, our needs and motives.

We can also freeze when it comes time for active listening if our partner has a problem with what we said. Keep the skill alive by active listening with your partner's minor disturbances. Just acknowledgement of their "hard day", "difficult encounter", "annoying commute" or "concern over too much to do" is a good way to connect in a sympathetic way, as well as good practice in responding with active listening.

Small Stuff

David Mace, who began Marriage Enrichment in 1972, encouraged Acting On The Pinch, meaning to speak about low level problems, before you get really upset. It's best to say something when you're just a little bit annoyed about things like messiness, disrespect or lateness instead of waiting too long and erupting in anger. The difficulty is choosing a good time so that our small complaint doesn't trigger a large response. If one of us is sick, tired, hungry or stressed, even a perfect I-message could be threatening. Be prepared to active listen if an I-message sparks a defensive reaction. I-messages can bring out guilt— sometimes we deserve a little guilt. Sometimes a simple problem can begin a long, exasperating dialog, other times an I-message will fix a difficulty in a jiffy.

Look for a good time to send an I-message. Before dinner is not usually the best time. Just before time for bed is not great either. Two I-messages at once is not the best and if your partner has had a tough day you may not get the results you'd like. Well, yes, this limits your options. Many couples plan time during the week to discuss schedules and air out any complaints, needs or concerns. If you realize that problems are part of the landscape of a relationship, it's natural to plan some time for weeding them out. Just ordinary garden variety maintenance.

Moderation

When I first learned about I-messages I wanted to solve all my problems at once and I began flinging I-messages at Jim and the children. This didn't work. It sounded like I was always irritated. Just one I-message a day or a week is best depending on the health of the relationship. Don't overdo a good thing. If there's tension then you accept and endure more discomfort for the sake of getting along better. A balancing of your comfort and congeniality. You can prioritize your annoyances.

You can use an I-message to begin again—a do-over—if you mistakenly began a discussion with criticism.

Don't expect that an I-message will always get you what you want. An I-message might solve a problem right away or open the door to discussion; hopefully it won't lead to a disagreement, but that can happen, too. Remember that switching to active listening is a way to control the damage.

One evening after dinner Jim went to lie on the couch and turned on the TV. Whatever he was watching prompted him to say, "People should talk about problems." I interpreted that as a "Sign" so I went in, loomed above him and gave him an I-message with no warning. Well, Jim felt attacked by that abruptness. I don't remember what my problem was, but I never got it solved because he was so upset by my approach.

My preferred method would be to tell Jim that I needed his help with a problem—when he was sitting up. I'd ask when would be a good time to address the difficulty. Then I'd say something about what was going well for us as a starter. Ater that I'd state my I-message, being ready to switch to active listening for objections, excuses, argument, hurt, defensiveness.

Thinking up the right I-message may seem like a great deal of work but having an issue peacefully resolved is worth some effort. Like good manners, kindness, and compassion, an I-message shows love and respect for your partner.

Other Uses

An I-message has other uses. One of the best ways to compliment someone is with a positive I-message. "I really liked your I-message. When you say what bothers you in such a gentle way I want to help you out."

Preventive I-messages help when there is a situation that has not gone well in the past and you want to warn about a similar event in the future. "Since we'll be having company for the weekend I'd be grateful for help with the garden and the meals." "I'd like to be on time for my banjo gig and would feel relieved if we can leave right at 7."

Benefits

I benefit from I-messages because I will think about the situation instead of reacting quickly. I calm down because I move from an emotional reaction to rational thinking about my needs. In choosing my words, I protected my partner and our relationship.

When I used a soft voice and told about my needs in the least demanding or harmful way, I enabled an accommodating response from Jim. The I-message just explained my needs and gave Jim a chance to tell me his needs, reasons and motives. We had a discussion instead of arguing.

Arguing would just give us a bad day, losing time that could be fun and enjoyable, losing peace of mind, and our warm connection.

We never felt like experts at I-messages. We were still working on them after practicing for 40 years in Marriage Enrichment. It was never a piece of cake. But worth the effort. Our relationship grew each time we settled a problem amicably. And, boy oh boy, were we happy!

Jim and Bea Strickland at a Banjo Banquet, 2010

Chapter 4

Watch Out For Teasing

You hear it on almost every TV sitcom. The funny insults are just part of the comedy. But it doesn't work so well in real life.

People hurl insults back and forth trying to be clever and joking. No one takes it seriously or do they?

Teasing can be harmful to relationships when the words said in a funny way would be insults and put-downs if said seriously. Yet teasing is quite prevalent in our culture. Parents tease their children, kids tease each other, and men joke with each other at work.

Teasing—we all do it from time to time. We're all victims once in a while. Sometimes it doesn't seem to bother us a bit. It can be funny, break the ice and lift a too serious mood. Sometimes, it really hurts and we remember the sting for a long time.

I used a new recipe, and it came out looking strange. The dinner was filled with laughter, but I never made that dish again, and I hesitate before trying new things.

Teasing seems to snowball. It begins slowly and each person wants to top the other's remark. The clever repartee picks up momentum and becomes an avalanche. I overheard two boys talking. First there was a small dig, "Is that your face, I thought it was a Halloween mask?" Then along came the bigger and better joke in retaliation. "Where were you when the brains were passed out, turkey, under the rug?" Two laughs, then the hitting started, and one complained. "I was only kidding, can't you take a joke?"

It seems to make anything acceptable if we say, "I was only joking." It's like a license to kill. I have an image of someone sticking in a knife and saying, "Don't bleed! I was just teasing." The way the routine goes, if you object, then the other person puts you down for being a poor sport or teases you for not liking to be teased.

Carl Rogers Said . . .

I asked the great psychologist, Carl Rogers, about the effects of teasing. He spoke at length about it. "Teasing was one of the major modes of communication in my family as a boy. You just had to develop a thick skin and give back as good as was sent. It wasn't until I got married and found how hurt my wife was when I would just toss off some sarcastic teasing remark, that I realized what armor plate we'd had to develop to live in that kind of atmosphere. I quite agree that most teasing has an underlying objective of hurting."

"I like humor," Rogers continued, "but that's quite different from teasing. The motivation of most drastic teasing is to hurt and that hurts relationships. It would be much better brought out in the open. If I don't like what you've done, it would be better to say so, in so many words, than to tease you or insult you in some subtle way. Teasing can have different motives. Usually they're unconscious motives, and that's what's too bad. If you are fully aware that you want to keep a person at a distance that's OK, but if you are teasing in order to do that and you're not aware, that's unfortunate."

Not So Funny

The effect of teasing is worse when a person's self esteem is low, and it's very difficult to judge the level of someone's self esteem. We all have hidden hot-spots, the sensitive places, that we don't advertise and may not be aware of. Once I teased a co-worker about some dumb thing he'd done and he got very quiet. I questioned him and found that my remark had bothered him. I thought he was smart, and that he knew that, but he didn't think he was so intelligent.

Unless we become aware of the consequences, we may continue to think teasing is harmless. Watch what happens after you've been teased. Monitor your feelings a while later. Sometimes it takes time for the bad feelings to surface. I may react well at the time I'm teased, but later I find myself remembering the teasing and wondering about the intent; or I become blue, and I don't know why.

I grew up in an atmosphere of teasing. My friends told me that I must learn to take a joke, lighten up, be able to laugh at myself. I tried. I decided that it must be a character fault, not being able to take being kidded, but I couldn't overcome it. I asked Jim if he would please stop teasing me because I never could tell whether I could take it, or whether I'd brood about what he said. He agreed to stop teasing me, and I was pleased that our interactions were less stressful and our whole relationship improved.

When I asked not to be teased, I thought I was the only weak, fragile person who couldn't take it, but I found more and more people who didn't like teasing either. I decided to quit teasing others. I was worried that life would become dull and conversations drab, but there are plenty of humorous moments in life. We can laugh a great deal without the risk of hurting others.

Teasing can interfere with the deepening of a relationship. When I know that someone teases, I have to guard what I say for fear I'll give them an opportunity to "get" me. I can never be sure that one of my goofs, weaknesses or vulnerabilities won't become material for getting a laugh. That certainly cuts down on spontaneity and keeps our friendship at a superficial level.

Motives For Teasing

What's behind the teasing? Why do we do it? A motive for teasing may be as simple as habit, or as complex as seeking power in a situation. A person who can make others laugh is the center of attention, while those being joked about are at the mercy of the teaser.

We tease others for a variety of reasons, some conscious and some unconscious. Sometimes we want to get a laugh, be funny or clever, stir things up and keep a conversation from becoming dull. Occasionally we'd like to get a message across without risk of confrontation. We can dig our spouse in front of company because there's safety in the group. "Alice is such a bad cook that even the dog gets sick on the leftovers!"

Many resentments can be hidden in jokes. Virginia Satir, world renowned family therapist and author, says, "Teasing is often unacknowledged hostility. It is an attempt to avoid responsibility for being honest. Teasing is often an effort to disclaim the presence of hostility and in effect, everyone loses."

Some people want to keep others from knowing them and being close, and will use teasing as a smoke screen. The joker keeps the spotlight, and no one ever hears about the problems and realities of his life.

Claude Steiner, a psychologist, says that teasing is brutal to children and a form of psychological abuse. "It's quite stressful for a child to be teased and lack the verbal ability to retaliate or be forbidden to do so".

Teasing, joking, and sarcasm, saying unkind things in a funny way, are accepted in our culture. It's a way of giving attention to each other, but what a damaging and cruel attempt at humor it is. We can all learn to become aware of the effects of teasing. We can find more direct, more gentle ways of confronting each other and more appropriate ways to bring laughter into our lives. We can say to others, "I'm uncomfortable with the teasing."

A poem I found that has an Ogden Nash flavor, sums up the whole irritating matter: "People need to be teased like a dog needs to have fleas."

CHAPTER 5

CONVERSATION

Conversation was one thing that was so rich and deep in Jim's and my relationship. I wish everyone could have conversations like that. Connecting, with positive conversations, leads to warmth, love and intimacy. We looked for subjects that were engaging for *both* of us. We used question lists from books, magazines or from Google. We talked during lunch, dinner, walks, and long drives; we talked to learn, to laugh, to love.

What Is It?

My definition of *real conversation* is when you connect with others: discussing an idea, engaging mindfully, understanding, sharing and building concepts together from a subject of interest to both. Conversation is two or more people talking and listening in turn, not judging, criticizing, correcting or bringing up problems. You have a goal of talking, you plan to spend time talking and listening, but the words come along spontaneously.

You may begin with one topic and branch out to others, like a tree. Each person feels safe to give an opinion, tell a story, share experiences, thoughts and ideas. Each person encourages the other with acknowledgement of what the other said. No precision is needed because you are not solving problems and each person has an opportunity to speak. Satisfying and positive conversation develops a true meeting of minds.

I always knew that I wanted to have conversations with Jim. College meant a great variety of topics to choose from; there were so many interactions in classes and socially, so we had chances for wide ranging conversation. After we were married it wasn't quite as easy to get a good conversation going spontaneously. The beginning, with choosing a subject, was difficult. Once we got going we could continue. I could always just chatter but I liked it when Jim participated and told me things about work, the world, philosophy or science. Jim had the idea that a person didn't talk unless there was a reason or a need. Then you were supposed to get to the point and stop. In business that was important but I wanted stories of Jim's life, what he believed in and what life was all about for him. Many years passed before he announced in front of a Marriage Enrichment group that he knew I liked conversation and that he was willing to cooperate, give details, his opinion, and take turns talking and listening. Once that was established as a norm we could begin with an idea and have fun with the interesting twists and turns. We could start with a question like: "What did you and your buddies do on hot summer afternoons as teenagers?". Our sources were varied; one time during a drive thru St Petersburg, FL, we saw some small churches with signs out front about the next sermon and I'd read them and one of us would pretend to give a sermon from that title. It was for fun and we'd laugh but then turn to discussing the topic for real: "Do Unto Others As You Would Have Them Do Unto You" or "Is Your House In Order?" or "Does Truth Lead YOU?"

Quick Disconnection

We don't always hear something in the way it's meant. The neurons go in the wrong direction. Sometimes we interpret something we hear in another way from the speaker's intention. We accidentally get it wrong. We jump to a conclusion. If there is tension in the relationship it's easy to get defensive and make the wrong assumption. Imagine a pre-party scene: He's in a helpful mood and says, "Can I do anything to help us get ready." Assuming that he is subtly criticizing, she replies, "I can't help it that I'm not ready. You're always complaining."

Because of stress, tiredness or prior tensions, we make quick judgements and think that what a person meant is different from what they were trying to say. It's discouraging when a good conversation won't just ignite like magic. There are so many factors and filters that get in between two minds. Sometimes it's a mystery and it may be best to wait for later to try again for an agreeable talk.

This is why active listening or acknowledgement is a very important step before jumping in with any comment of your own when you instantly disagree or bristle. When you hear an accusation, just pause and make sure of what your partner meant. Just repeating a bit of what you thought you understood, can clear things up. If it wasn't a criticism, fine. If it was, maybe the other person will explain, correct themselves or back off. For discussion: When are the times when you are likely to feel vulnerable and mis-hear a comment? Before company arrives? Just after work? Holidays? Getting ready for travel? Planning for something? Before dinner?

Missing What's Said

Couples don't always hear, notice and realize when important words are said. Sometimes a whole group can miss a significant statement. Jim and I were at a Board meeting of Better Marriages when there was a discussion of hiring a new executive director. David Catron stated that he and Sarah were wondering if Sarah might do that job, just gratis. No one acknowledged his remark until Jim spoke up and said, "Wait just a moment, I believe David has given us a possible solution and we didn't really hear him." Sarah Catron subsequently became the director and served Better Marriages marvelously. If Jim had not heard and pointed out what David was suggesting, David and Sarah might have thought the Board didn't want to discuss the possibility and the group might have gone on to some other decision. How many times have other suggestions been passed over from lack of listening, a pause, acknowledgement, and discussion? We get in a hurry, "we listen too fast without hearing". The worst thing I ever overheard was when a man was describing his wife's death and said it was 'bizarre'. The listener hurried to explain that death was not 'bizarre' and said, "You must reframe your thoughts." I would guess that the man was trying to describe his feelings and that when the 'listener' interrupted and picked the one word to correct, it must have been painful.

Connection vs Interruption

One person's bid for connection may be the receiver's interruption. It's like entering without knocking. If you are busy doing something: reading, writing, doing taxes, sudoku, homework; no matter if it's trivial or important, it can feel like an intrusion when someone interrupts you without asking permission or apologizing. It may startle you or you may lose your train of thought. For Jim and me it was like a little syndrome that we didn't recognize at first. When Jim would come to say something to me and I was in the middle of writing or reading, I would feel disrespected first and then guilty for not being receptive to Jim. He would feel hurt if I complained. We were both guilty of seeking each other out and then just starting to talk. We may have even had the other's interest at heart. I might have something that I thought would entertain Jim. When he showed irritation at my bid for connection I would feel rejected. Neither of us would feel good about approaching each other for awhile. We finally got this straightened out for ourselves and then it stopped being an irritant. We talked about it very gingerly and recognized the problem as feeling interrupted, unimportant or disrespected. The attempt to talk might have been a compliment but it didn't feel that way. We devised our own solution: we'd wait a moment to be acknowledged, then ask if it was a good time to talk.

'Could we talk?' or 'Excuse me for interrupting.' or 'When you have a moment…' All these signal the respect you have for your partner's pursuits and activities. The preliminary request shows that I know that you and your time are important. What would be a good starter for you and your partner in that situation?

Shifting Attention

There's a difference in our thinking and attention when we're working alone and the times when we're focused on the other person and having a conversation. It takes a real switch from one kind of concentration to another. I thought Jim did that rather quickly. I'd go sit in the big black fake leather chair in his office and wait until he finished on the computer and turned around, then I'd ask if it was OK to talk now.

When you've been reading or writing and you get interrupted by a question from your partner, it takes time to adjust to listening mode. It's a skill to learn—to be able to go from "attending to business and tasks and your own inner world" to "warm, interested, friendly listener" in a short period of time. If you've just come home from work it's a shock to hear complaints or hear the children arguing. The transition may take place in different parts of our brains. What do you do to adjust your attention? As a couple we need to be aware that when we want to talk to our spouse that they may be in task mode and need a moment to change to conversation mode.

Too Silly To Discuss?

There are times when one person wants to talk about something that the other thinks is silly, stupid or trivial and not worth time spent in conversation. Jim and I came to an agreement that if one of us wanted to talk about an issue that we'd make time to talk and not consider it a waste of time. That led to some interesting moments like the looonnngg discussion we had in line at the Golden Horseshoe Saloon at DisneyWorld. We'd had an agreement with our sons and their wives the night before, that we would meet at the Saloon at 11:30. When we saw the doors to the saloon were beginning to open it meant that we'd be going in and our chance to meet up with our family would become more difficult. I was in favor of going in because the family might never show up and Jim wanted to wait even if it meant not going into the Saloon. It took us way more than a sentence to resolve this. We decided I would go in and save a table if I could and Jim would wait. It was an amicable process but I'm sure those very quiet people near us were rolling their eyes. Just in time our son came, said he didn't want a hot dog for breakfast and we agreed on another meeting time and place. Our agreement to talk about the silly and trivial saved us from pent up anger, disappointment and from that standpoint it was not a waste of time. I think that if there were a long series of conversations about minor problems, that might become a sore point, but for us occasional working out of minutiae was well worth the time.

Sharing Air Time

Sometimes people get 'on a roll' and can keep talking for way too long. A student in my Couple's Communication class reported that he'd really listened. Listened to his wife for two hours. That poor guy. That's an hour and forty minutes too long!

In most relationships there will be one person that talks more than the other and it's good to find out if that's comfortable for both. I talked more than Jim but he was fine with that. And when he did talk I tried to listen.

Having a real conversation means taking turns. One person talks, one listens and then responds appropriately to what the other has said. It's not a competition, you don't have to hurry to make points. The goal is to connect, to give each other attention, good eye contact. Togetherness. Take turns. It's hard to decide what is a reasonable length of time to keep talking but people generally want to have some time to talk and be listened to. As much as possible, let the person talk rather than interrupting them, though if you are adding a short phrase that echoes what the other is saying, it may feel encouraging to the talker.

When we interrupt, change the subject or insist on our viewpoint we vie for power in a conversation. Then we're just like kids saying, "Me, Me!" Whenever someone else is the focus we want it back on us even if we don't have anything to say. All of a sudden we're in a hurry? Also, we start talking without remembering the goal of satisfaction for both people. We stop listening. We just do it the old way, maybe what was modeled at the dinner table when we were kids.

If we could only remember the quote from David Augsburger, "Being listened to is so close to being loved that most people don't know the difference."

Ask and Listen. Whatever the reason, it maybe nervousness or a racing brain, I have a tendency to ask someone a question and, while they are mulling over an answer, I start talking about something else.

> "The art of conversation consists as much in listening politely, as in talking agreeably." – Atwell

Connecting Techniques

Each of these ideas can be used as a conversation with your partner as you explore what makes you feel listened to and enhances your experience of conversation. Some conversation aids are subtle but not everyone likes all the ideas. Head nodding and saying "uh huh" could be a turn-off to one person or encouraging to another. Have a conversation to find out what your partner likes.

Eye Contact

Look at your partner's eyes or face. Eye Contact is such an easy thing to do but also easy to forget. When we are preoccupied with a task or worried about something we tend to look off into the distance or down. Our brains are wired to notice peripheral movement and it's easy to get distracted from listening, by a squirrel out the window or people moving around in the background and then we shift our gaze and often, our attention.

Consciously looking at our partner, not staring, but friendly eye contact, eyes medium wide, relaxed face, minus frowns or downturned mouth, shows great interest, gives reassurance and warmth in a conversation.

I remember John Gray giving an exercise at a seminar saying, "Look at your partner as though everything they are saying is incredibly important and marvelously interesting. Then they will feel important and interesting."

Gazing into your partner's eyes is easiest when you are doing the listening. It's hard to keep eye contact when talking. During your time to talk you may look away at times because it's a normal reaction to look up or to the side when recalling a memory or an idea.

When Jim and I went to a restaurant for a cozy dinner we deliberately sat across from each other to facilitate eye contact. It's natural to look forward. Then, since we both knew we liked eye contact, we were intentional about it. It helped give us each a sense of intimacy, importance and satisfying rapport.

Respond to Comments

Very little of my education was focused on having a good conversation. I am saying "very little" when I really mean that I was never given any education in how to converse with someone. It was all about picking it up from the grownups, then trial and error with a great many errors. Then came Parent Effectiveness Training and I learned about active listening and realized that responding and acknowledging what a person says, is important a lot more often than just in emotional turmoil and problem solving.

The book *Connections*, by Sherod Miller, talks about the process of conversation and *Communicycles*. It's a simple matter of one person speaking and the other responding. If you say, "What time is it?" And your partner replies, "8 PM". And you say, "Thanks". Then you've completed a Communicycle. To be satisfying, a conversation needs that completed cycle. You've asked and been answered. Also, when you make a bid for connection you want a friendly response. It hurts to be ignored or put down by words or tone of voice. You may have many rounds in your cycle or just a few, depending on the goal of the visit. The talk is usually finished when the initiator feels the process is complete. Miller says, "People who say they don't communicate, often really mean they don't finish communicycles."

Repeat Happy Memories

Don't stop your partner from telling the happy old memories just because you've heard that story before. Encourage your partner. It's good for you both to retell the fun, happy, warm moments of your past. It gives joy to the teller and the listener. It says, "LOOK at that good time. Don't we have a history of joy with much more to come!" You have stories of great restaurants, travel, fun times with the children, times when you were impressed and awed, tender moments when you first knew you were in love or expressed that passion. Tell and enjoy those stories again and again. Indulge yourself in repeating and rehearing.

Speak From Your Experience

It's OK to use 'I' and to disclose yourself, to speak from first person. Long ago we were told not use 'I' very often. Maybe it was thought to be selfish or narcissistic. But often when we open a conversation it helps to give others the idea of our subject by being specific about our experience. "I went for a walk today and looked at the sky. It gave me such peace of mind. What relaxes you and gives you peace of mind?" Ask specific questions. It's okay to ask for information - "Tell me about your hobby; why is it fun for you?"

Speak with Expression

Change your tone of voice, rate, tempo, and inflection from time to time. Let your face and voice be animated. Remember to breathe deeply often enough so that you have some energy behind your words. I have trouble keeping people awake so I wave my arms around. I used to have a meditation group and I often did put them to sleep.

Agree

Agreeableness is a positive personality trait that can be developed. Agree with what your partner says as often as possible, because as soon as a "no" or opposite statement is said, the conversation can become argumentative or just come to a halt. You encourage defensiveness when you disagree. You can find some part of your partner's statement to agree with. Or you can active listen to their point of view which is not disagreeing. At least this can slow down the interaction.

Yes, And . . .

After acknowledging, with brief active listening, to your partner's idea, it's often affirming to add to the idea. In an Improv Theatre, where actors make up a scene as they go along, the rule is "Yes, and..." The actors validate rather than correct, criticize or negate what their partner has just said. Actor One says, "The political scene sure is wild." Actor Two, "Yes, it's wild and so interesting, we don't know what's next." The word "yes" is an enhancer—it validates what your partner said. Then you can add your idea. It helps keep the conversation going instead of shutting it off.

I didn't realize how much it disturbed a good conversation to bring up a problem or criticism in the middle. Something would trigger me to remember an issue or some negative thing from the past and I'd bring it up when we were enjoying ourselves. Even a small problem would cause a hurt or an angry response. Evidently we relax and are more open and trusting when we're having an easy talk. Then it's jolt to insert the problem. So wait for another time or ask veeerrry carefully for a change in subject to talk about corrections from the past, issues or problems. The same is true of 'subtly' inserting a little jab of criticism about faults. That hurts.

> "The real art of conversation is not only to say the right thing at the right place but to leave unsaid the wrong thing at the tempting moment." – Dorothy Neville.

Stories

We live our lives as a series of stories. Stories are fun but don't make them too long, and when you do tell a story be ready for others to be triggered to tell their own story. They may get inspired and just start talking which interrupts your story. You may want to let them talk and let go of your own story because all of a sudden you have interesting interaction. Keep your sense of humor because conversations don't always follow the path you started and for most casual conversations it's best to have preferences about how it should go but not specific expectations. If it's a group with a specific goal then keeping to the topic is more important.

What's Happening

Read a lot - keep up with your newspaper. Or don't. Do the opposite and make social time an opportunity to keep up with current events.

What to Talk About?

Intentional positive conversation helps you to be happier. It's the way to talk without criticizing, correcting or complaining about your partner. There are subjects that you can discuss that don't require judgements. Books, movies, TV, sports,art, music, philosphy, values. You just give your thoughts. It's not a rant or a tirade. You aren't trying to win anything, be right or gain superiority. You're just telling about your view of life or pondering some possibility. What do you think...? Do you think that if you are happier that maybe you are nicer to your partner? Do you think that feeling happy might help you be more accepting of (real or imagined) flaws of your partner? It is very possible that these are subtle benefits of being happy and having a connecting conversation. When you are having a mutually satisfying conversation you both are accepting and loving each other and not thinking about faults. How pleasant.

Focus on the positive aspects of life in general and talk about what's good about your lives. For conversations at dinner or in the car ask: What are some of the ways that I encourage, promote, or help you be happy? Did you do anything today that contributed to your own happiness? What does happiness mean to you?

Little things mean a lot—Change one thing for the good and there can be a whole chain of subsequent happy results. Just deciding to explore various new topics of conversation might give your relationship a boost.

What do you consider interesting, exciting, satisfying or meaningful conversation? What constitutes an important discussion to your partner? It could be meaningful just to talk about what each of you think is fun to talk about.

Conversation is bonding, it helps us learn about each others' thoughts, about the past, about our fears, our wishes, hopes, and dreams. We feel less alone. We grow. We connect. Happily. I've forgotten the words and what we ate for dinner but I'll never forget how good it felt to talk to each other.

In Mendocino after our connecting-discussion about soup.

Jim and Bea dialoging at the
2015 Better Marriages Conference

Chapter 6

Importance of Conversation

> Our relationships may be the most important aspect of our lives. We build, maintain, retain and enrich our relationships through conversation. We know each other through a series of conversations A relationship means ongoing, talking together. Conversation is the pathway to an intimate relationship.
> – Bea and Jim Strickland

The best part of our lives are our relationships. Since each relationship is lived one conversation at a time; relationships are made, strengthened or hurt through talk. The moments we spend with our loved ones in meaningful conversation can be very precious. Make conversation a value in your life.

Conversations with a plan or an agenda are much more satisfying and meaningful.

One myth about sex is that it should be spontaneous and people believe conversation, too, should just happen on the spot—magically the words will come. Or, that if it's planned, it isn't authentic or right. But subjects that are entertaining for both people enhance conversation. Those topics ought to be consciously thought about before you have an opportunity to talk to each other.

There are times when you need to discuss business, problems, household chores. There are times when you just want to be quiet together. There are times when you are just too tired or not feeling well and don't want to talk. But it's practically a sin to let a golden opportunity go by when you could exchange ideas about values, science, art, music, feelings, or the meaning of life. Here's your topic for today. "How do you define hope? What is the difference between wishful thinking and what you can really have?"

> Each person's life is lived as a series of conversations.
> – Deborah Tannen

Bids For Connection

We want to connect in conversation because it feels good. John Gottman, professor of psychology and researcher in marital stability, originated the concept of bids for connection. There are many reasons why we want to connect with others and have social contact. It's not as much fun to be a hermit, although we all need time alone. Some theories maintain that ancient peoples had a need for safety in numbers, could share food, help each other, and teach ways to survive. Whatever the old reasons are, today we crave social acceptance, want the company and comfort of others, and like the attention we get. We say or do something to gain attention. Usually we don't just say, "Let's talk"; although that would be a good idea. We make some kind of bid for attention and connection. If we are aware that we are social beings, needing contact, then we can realize that others are also wanting support, comfort and that they seek our attention. When you hear a bid for connection—a question, comment or statement from your partner—you have three choices: one to answer in a friendly, empathic manner; two to ignore or change the subject; or three to argue, criticize or be sarcastic.

We had never thought of communication just that way. When Jim and I heard that simple formula—person one has a desire for connection, person two has three options: be friendly, ignore or be argumentative—we were delighted by the simplicity and truth of this explanation. We were both surprised at how obvious it was that, of course, we wanted to be friendly.

Harmony and the close warm feeling we get when someone is understanding us, cooperating, or agreeing is the joy of a relationship. Whether we call it rapport or togetherness or being on the same page/wavelength, it feels satisfying and safe.

I used to ask Jim, "What do you want for dinner?" Or "What do you want to do today?" Trying to be generous he would answer, "Anything you want." I would hear this as, "He doesn't care to talk to me."

My question had more to do with an (often unconscious) desire for conversation than for a food or activity answer. I was making a bid for connection when I asked the question about dinner. Jim and I learned that I was looking for involvement and that wonderful feeling of togetherness, rather than a fact. Later I became aware of my need for conversation as a connection and could just ask Jim if we could talk. He'd respond because he knew it was a gift to me.

We all want some times of closeness with our partners. I wanted Jim to engage every now and then — even in trivial matters. (Not all the time, he needed time by himself.)

It wasn't until we went to Mendocino one time and were foraging for food at the little grocery store that I recognized what was truly satisfying. We were having a deep discussion about the merits of Progresso versus Campbell soup and we both realized that we were listening and concentrating on each other and it was fun! Very trivial, but we were engaged with each other.

The soup wasn't important; it was the experience of that moment of connection and concentration on each other that was valuable. I don't even remember what soup we chose but I still remember the feeling of the conversation. It's the contact, the give and take, talking it over, bonding, connecting.

Conversation ought to make both parties feel heard, satisfied and happy. What fun it is when you've 'had a moment' being engaged with each other in a mutually agreeable conversation. Look for more than chit-chat, passing time, gossiping and 'pass-the-salt'.

Cycles

Very much related to bids for connection, are the cycles that seem to occur in a relationship, lasting from hours to weeks.

In all your relationships you go around in cycles of *empathy, withdrawal or antagonism.* If it's a time of empathy then you're connected, listening, understanding each other, feeling warm and affectionate with your loved one. That's what we all want.

If you're withdrawn it may be that you just need time by yourself. Sometimes you don't feel particularly friendly or you have a problem you are working out in your head and not ready to talk about. Or you are tired and a tired brain does not move from one happy thought to another.

If it's a cycle of antagonism you may be openly hostile and verbal about it or quietly irritated about something and non-communicative. It may be an issue with your partner or an outside problem.

Jim and I talked about the cycles and knew we wanted to feel connected. We'd go back and forth; in and out of the cycles. We knew that it was natural and normal, but having a goal of being best friends encouraged us to inquire when the other was not sounding loving. Our goal became, "How fast can we get back to being friends?" Then we could talk about feelings, what was happening and get to the empathy cycle again.[1]

Store up credit in your love bank. Think of ways to be affirming and affectionate. Say caring and compassionate things to your partner. Include lots of compliments and affirmation in your conversation. You are a comment away from a warm, loving relationship.

Conversation is for making each other feel good; contributing to the topic in a positive way shows interest; listening carefully

---

1 See www.danwile.com

indicates that all thoughts and opinions are valued. It all says, "*You* are important to me!"

> "The true spirit of conversation consists more in bringing out the cleverness of others than in showing a great deal of it yourself; he who goes away pleased with himself and his own wit is also greatly pleased with you." – Jean de La Bruyère

Intimacy

Intimacy is the deepest feeling of connection. Conversation ought to be about bringing two people closer to one another. First recognize that positive conversation is a value, benefit and desirable. Then, the conversation should be a mutually enjoyable interchange. You take turns talking and active listening. The careful attending to each other leads to feelings of being respected and understood. After understanding comes compassion and then love and intimacy. Intimacy is one of the most important reasons for meaningful conversation.

Intimacy is that great feeling of warmth and closeness, being involved with each other, one of the best things about a relationship. When you take turns talking and listening to each other, making an intentional effort to focus just on your partner, you feed your relationship. Let your partner know you'd like more closeness. Look for a few moments a day or a half hour every couple of days. Talk about hopes, dreams, fears, and triumphs. Ask, "What was the best and worst part of your day?" The payoff is happiness and satisfaction for both of you.

Sometimes your mood, your environment and activities will mean that you can connect readily and jump easily into intimacy. Other times it takes comments, questions, validation, affirmation, compliments—a warm-up—to get to a place of harmony and closeness.

> "When marrying, ask yourself this question: Do you believe that you will be able to converse well with this person into your old age? Everything else in marriage is transitory."
> – Friedrich Nietzsche

Jim and Bea at a Better Marriages Retreat

Chapter 7

A Page or Two About Sex

How could there be so many books and magazine articles about sex and have it remain such a mystery? There have been times in my life when I thought I had an understanding of my own sex life and how to do it. Then that confidence would disappear.

My cousin Steve gave me a nickel for kissing my cousin John when I was about 10. When I proudly told my father about it he said, "Don't ever tell me that again." So I never told him again. Never kissed and told. But I really liked kissing. And now I'm telling.

Jim's and my earliest relationship was pretty passionate with kissing and what we called petting — but it was the 50's — so there was no sexual intercourse. Except once when our desire really built up after 2 years of wanting more.

Early Marriage

We married young — 18 and 20. It was a wonderfully sex filled marriage for a while until the stress of work and children intervened and our carefulness and kindness to each other declined. Resentments built and sex was still exciting when it happened but there were more and more reasons not to engage.

When we moved to Nashville in our 20th year of marriage,

we became involved in Marriage Enrichment and began a whole new marriage: wanting to move closer to each other and have the best relationship possible. We started talking about sex for the first time. We had spoken sexy things during sex but never about sex, after or before, as a topic to discuss. Somehow I thought it might lose its magic if we talked about what we did. So, with Marriage Enrichment, our sex life improved along with day to day life together. Talking about what we did, and asking about changes we should make for each other, helped us grow and and enjoy sex much more.

We tried new things, a little soft porn, not waiting too late at night to have sex and with little bits of trial and error, sex became better and better, in a two steps forward and one backward, fashion. We'd think we had it just right and then some little glitch would occur and it was time to figure it out again.

We were both careful not to make fun of each other's bodies in any way. I knew a woman whose husband called her breasts "fried eggs" and she was never comfortable with her body.

Jim's drive stayed quite strong but mine waned somewhat. About 22 years ago I wanted to do something about my lack of enthusiasm. I invited some women from our Marriage Enrichment groups to come and talk about sex at a day-long seminar in my home with pizza for lunch. About 17 women responded and we talked about our feelings about sex compared to our husbands' wants and needs.

There were a couple of women who wanted sexual intercourse more than their husbands but most of us were on the side of feeling finicky and ambivalent about sex. There were all kinds of issues. Timing – meaning he's too fast about everything, wanting too much too soon. Not in the mood – meaning she's ready to go to sleep and he suggests sex or starts being amorous. Cleanliness – she thinks they both need a shower. Chores – not being able to quit work to have sex.

Nothing was resolved on that day or in a subsequent workshop. Then three of us decided we'd like to figure it all out and get to some answers for having more positive feelings about sex. We wanted to know why we were reluctant, how to get to harmony with our husbands and be at peace with the problem of the difference in sexual desire with our husbands. We wanted to want to have sex. We three began meeting about once a month to talk about our sex lives and learn from each other or just 'talk it out' for some relief. This was 22 years ago and we still meet. We've added two more women. Our conclusions are few and weak, though our suggestions are numerous and our laughter delightful.

I decided that I wanted to meet Jim's wants and have sex more frequently. At least 3 times a week. Jim was delighted and grateful that I wanted to do that and was overboard-eager to help me want and enjoy sex. For a while we would enjoy sex and feel confident about our practice.

Then there would be some interruption: physical, mental or emotional and we would be at odds and have to work on why we weren't compatible and connecting. Sometimes it just resolved without any problem solving and other times we would change some aspect that led to smoother sex. In our 60s Viagra took care of one problem. But it seemed to be an ongoing mystery. Why was sex such ecstacy at times and then other times a problem?

One, Two, Three, Foreplay

One solution came in the form of our Marriage Enrichment idea about *one, two, three fourplay*. Jim and I presented a program about sex for Saturday evening of our Marriage Enrichment retreat. Our idea was that we need something leading up to foreplay to encourage a desire for sex in the first place. Something better than "Let's have sex." What would that be?

Working backwards, if foreplay is sexual activity that precedes intercourse, like kissing, fondling naked body parts, fingering, talking dirty, then what needs to happen before that to want to get to foreplay?

For the Marriage Enrichment retreat we divided into small groups to talk about what men wanted, what women wanted, and what led to a desire for sex. Three-play was described as flirting, hugging, kissing, sexual suggestion, innuendo or just asking for sex.

Then what came before that? What was two-play? Well, when a partner talks and listens and responds to bids for attention and gives affection without expectation of sex, it makes us feel valued and loved. That intimate connection, the loved and cared-for feeling translates to a desire for more closeness which leads to three-play.

And one-play? What did the little groups decide was the forerunner to two-play? Respect, courtesy, manners, helping, doing little favors, paying attention, lots of affection, smiles, apologies for slights, forgiveness. All the nice friendship attributes. Every day. All the time. It was kind of a revelation for us. That being nice today leads to more sex tomorrow, it certainly led to more willingness for me. I wonder if couples who are nice to each other on a regular basis have more sex? What do you think?

I think that men can often override a little disconnection because their testosterone level is higher and therefore their sex drive is stronger. Not always though. If I hurt Jim's feelings in some way, he might be a bit standoffish until we got it straightened out. Really, though, I was the one who wanted lots of affection and attention all the time. I'm more of an extrovert. As long as I gave Jim lots of alone time, since he was an introvert, he liked the affection and enjoyed our conversations, too.

Who Initiates Sex?

Our tiny sex discussion group thought that it was probably the man in most cases that wants the most sex and will ask or indicate by his friendliness that he's wanting sex.

When Jim and I realized that my desire wasn't strong any more—but of course I adored him and that it had nothing to do with how much I loved him—then we worked on some ideas. We decided that we could plan to have sex, set dates for three times a week, have a romantic dinner with candles and wine and cook together. Or we'd go out for dinner. But we rarely ever waited til 10 PM for sex. Both of us were too tired. This planning all occurred in our later 40s, 50s, 60s and in our 70s until Jim died at 79. Our children were not at home any more; we were free to plan an evening the way we wanted.

Contributions To Sex

I guess since Jim wanted sex more than I did, he also contributed the most toward our evenings. He wasn't thrilled with cooking but we made marvelous dinners together like Lobster Mornay, Crab Crepes, Cheese Fondue. Jim liked Costco so he'd shop, too. He always showered. He was more of a dominant so he directed sex and pushed me for more. I would wear cute little outfits, dresses, negligees, nighties and high heels and net stockings for him. He would coax me and compliment. We tried a few sex board games. We had role plays with Jim being Dr Stryker, the psychologist, who helped me "realize my full sexual potential." It was exciting. I was always less eager than Jim, but I heard a comedian say, "Women never want sex but they like it when they're doing it." That seemed to be the way it was. Now it seems to be recognized that for women, desire often follows physical arousal. I was reticent to begin with, worrying that I wouldn't get aroused and would spoil the experience for Jim, but then as we went along in the evening and the process, I got into it.

Now it's been a year since Jim died and I seem not to need any sex and that kind of surprises me. I am still a member of my women's group discussing sex every 4-6 weeks. Talking about it is fun for me. Reading novels with sex included is enjoyable. Maybe it's a matter of age, being 79 means I physically don't need sex. But it's still an interesting subject. I'm curious about how others handle the topic and what kind of an issue it is—or isn't. Most of the women I've talked to about sex say they aren't a bit eager but I do know one couple at 87 and 91 who still have an active sex life. They're late-in-life unmarried lovers.

If both people feel the same about sex, either they both enjoy it or both don't care, then it should not be any problem, no matter how many books say that you should want and have sex at least once a week. Many of the books about sex and magazine articles increased my guilt. I heard a great comment: "What if sex is something that some people desire more than others and, like playing golf, it might be your passion but it isn't mine. I have sex with him because I want to please him and give that to him but I don't have to like it. Thank heavens that the part of sex I enjoy least is just 10 minutes long. If he wanted me to play golf with him, I don't think our marriage would last."

John Price enjoyed my poem in the preface and rewrote it in Iambic Pentameter.

Side By Side

Two trees still standing there.
We liked those trees
And mused about their age.
Had they too stood
For sixty years as we had, side by side?
We smiled about their faith to keep alive
Throughout the winter times, and hope for spring
And soft new leaves.
Their steady presence gave
Us hope as well, connected to those trees.
The memories of sixty years we shared
Are comfort to me now, and in my heart
We too are standing there, still side by side.

Appendix A

Extra Materials

Blocks to Listening

These are things that discourage a person from expressing emotion or talking about a problem. The things that stop communication when there is anger, sadness, fear or worry are:

Advice and Orders. Giving solutions, telling the person what they should do. Commanding them to change. Examples, (all unwelcome when someone needs to be listened to):

Examples
You must . . .
ought to . . .
should . . .
have to . . .
Ignore it. Forget it. Forgive.
Have patience. Don't worry.
Think about the good things.
Use I Messages.

If you would listen first and respond with paraphrasing, maybe they will feel heard and be willing to listen to you.

Judgement. Giving reasons why the person is in the situation.

Telling a person what is wrong with them or their thinking, feelings, conclusions or solutions.

Examples
If you had only listened in the first place.
You didn't use I Messages and speak from your experience.

Blaming. Criticizing. Naming the faults, telling them that it's their fault and how wrong they are.

Examples
The reason this happened is because you don't take the time to show them you understand their point of view.
You started it when you argued and became defensive instead of listening first.
You have no patience . . .

Name calling. Labeling. Admonishing by saying, 'stupid, crybaby, silly, wimp, fool, loser, quitter, cheater, jerk, too emotional'

Threatening. Warning.

Examples
If you don't really listen then things will just escalate.
If you don't use I Messages and tell your problem then they will over re-act.

Disagreeing.

Examples
You are seeing this all wrong.
Here is the real problem and answer.

Praising. Although not as much of a conversation stopper, when you extol the person's virtues it doesn't help them express their feelings.

Examples
You are so loving.
You were kind to her.
You're so smart.

Sympathy. Saying, 'I'm so sorry.' is kindly meant but often doesn't encourage more from the other person as does *active listening*.

Cheering them up, moralizing. Pointing out that things aren't so bad. Trying to talk them out of their feelings.

Examples
Look on the bright side.
It's not all that bad.
You'll be fine. Everything will be OK.
You worry too much.

Encouraging Talk

To help and encourage someone to talk when they are emotional or have a problem and you want to help in the best way and you'd like them to feel the most comfortable about expressing their problem. It would be helpful to listen and let them come to a solution.

Better for Listening and letting the other person talk are:

Examples
Would you like to talk about it?
I'd be glad to listen if you want to say more.
Tell me more.

Body Language that indicates that you are listening:

Examples
Turning toward the person. Eye contact.
Assuming a position that mirrors the speaker.
Sitting at their eye level or below so as not to look dictatorial or superior.

Sounds. Empathic words, sounds:

Examples
Oh, Aww, Umm

Active listening is the best way to listen if someone is emotional, has a problem or has something important to convey.

Conversation Negatives

If you start your response to your partner with "but", "no" or "you're wrong" the results can be painful:

BUT	the killer, "but", negates everything your partner said.
NO	the conversation stopper or argument starter. 'No' says, "You're wrong."

Finishing sentences and words. I welcome help because often the other person knows what I mean and can supply the word. As long as I see that they seem interested, that helps me. Others consider the 'help' as an interruption. How does your partner feel about that?

Frowning. Sometimes our listening face may not look approving and encouraging. I had a drama teacher who was one of the nicest people in the world but when she was concentrating on what you were saying she looked like she completely disapproved.

Being too general - "How's your life?"

Correction and criticism shut down disclosure. We want our loved ones to be right and truthful so sometimes we correct them just to be helpful. It probably doesn't matter, just let them tell the story their way. It may not be as accurate as your version but the correction is annoying to the speaker and the listeners.

Examples
Arguing, lecturing, ranting.
Spreading unpleasant gossip
Asking, "How much money did that cost?"
Producing guilt.
Putting your partner or yourself down
Sarcasm
Teasing
Asking obvious questions -"Did you get your hair cut?"
Saying "Really?" like "I doubt it."

Being sick, tired or hungry and expecting a great conversation.
Talking too long at one time.
"Of course" (implied 'stupid')

Humor: Negative and Positive

From The Humor Project [1]

Laughing At Others: Toxic Humor

You know how it is when you come home from a party and even though you laughed a lot you have an ache – not from all the wine and food but because there were hurtful things said in the guise of humor. To you and to your friends. Lots of little zingers. Ouch.

1. Based on contempt and insensitivity
2. Outcome: destroys confidence through put-downs
3. Excludes some people
4. A person does not choose to be made fun of
5. Abusing, offends others
6. Sarcastic and mean
7. Outcome: divides people
8. Leads to a one-downsmanship cycle
9. Reinforces stereotypes by singling out a particular group as the "butt"
10. Goes for the jugular vein

Laughing With Others: Nourishing Humor

1. Based on caring and empathy
2. Outcome: builds confidence

[1] See http://www.humorproject.com/

3. Involves people in the fun
4. A person chooses to be the "butt" of a joke (as in "laughing at yourself")
5. Amusing: invites people to laugh
6. Supportive and clean
7. Outcome: brings people closer
8. Leads to positive repartee
9. Pokes fun at universal human foibles
10. Goes for the jocular vein

> "The time has come", the walrus said "to talk of many things: of shoes and ships and sealing wax, of cabbages and kings and why the sea is boiling hot and whether pigs have wings." – Lewis Carroll

You can combine Subjects and Key Words.

Subjects		
Animals	Art	Books
Childhood	Children	Cooking
Current events	Food	Hobbies
History	Holidays	Inventions
Meals	Movies	Music
Science	Sports	Television
Travel	Weather	

Key words		
Best	Compare	Contrast
Dislike	Earliest	Favorite
First	How	Like
Most	What	When
Who	Why	

Getting a Conversation Started

There are two kinds of conversations: those that you sort of fall into and those that are planned. If you fall into a conversation, then just keep it going. But, if you are having problems getting started here are some ideas.

Ask a question from the list below

Read an article in the newspaper, summarize it and ask questions about how your partner feels about it. Pick a subject and a key word from the lists above and form a question.

Use the "dart" technique. Open a book or magazine at random, point to a place on the page at random then read a few words and use that as a springboard.

Keeping a Conversation Going

Use questions — especially open ended questions. The simplest, easiest-to-remember conversation tools are: "Tell me more" and "How did you feel about that?" Don't worry about occasional pauses.

> A man uses "report talk" to convey information and self-importance; while a woman uses "rapport talk" to try to establish intimacy and connection. – Deborah Tannen

Conversing with Questions

The following is excerpted from *Conversationally Speaking* by Alan Garner. There are two types of questions you can pose: closed-ended and open-ended.

Closed-Ended Questions

Closed-ended questions are like true-false or multiple-choice questions in that they request only a one- or two-word reply.

Examples
Where are you from?
Shall we have dinner tonight at 5:30, 6, or 6:30?
Do you think all atomic power plants should be shut down?

Closed-ended questions are valuable for getting others to disclose specific facts about themselves that you may wish to explore in greater detail ("I was born in Detroit, but I grew up in Huntsville, Alabama.") and for getting them to state definite positions ("Six o'clock is fine with me." "I don't want those we have shut down, but I don't favor building any more either.").

While they have a definite role to play, closed-ended questions lead to dull conversations followed by awkward silences when they are used exclusively. People asked a series of closed-ended questions soon feel like they're being interrogated by the FBI.

Open-ended Questions

You have to follow up your closed-ended questions with open-ended ones if you want to keep your conversations going and allow them to achieve greater interest and depth. Open-ended questions are like essay questions in that they promote answers of more than a word or two. They ask for explanations and elaboration, while showing your conversational partners (much to their delight!) that you are so interested in what they have said that you want to know more.

The following lists should help you in starting off your questions:

Closed-Ended	Both	Open-ended
Are?	What?	How?
Do?		Why?
Who?		In what way?
When?		
Where?		
Which?		

You may have speculated that some people would probably answer many of the closed-ended questions you've read in open-ended ways. While this is true, your conversational partners are likely to answer open-ended questions at consistently greater length because they actively encourage speaking freely. When you ask open-ended questions, others can relax, knowing that you want them to get involved and express themselves fully.

Asking Questions That Are Too Open-ended

Midge, the wife of a university administrator, said that she's becoming bored with her life. Why? "Because all day long all I've got for company is a three-year-old and an infant. So when Mel comes home and I ask him, 'How'd it go today?' I really want to know. But what does he say? 'Oh, the usual.' Then he turns on the TV and that's that."

Midge had been making several simple errors: First, her inquiry was too broad in scope. Asking questions is like turning faucets in that the more open they are, the more response you get—up to a point. Very open-ended questions like Midge's (as well as "What's new?" "What have you been up to lately?" and "Tell me about yourself.") would require so much effort and time to answer that most people give up without even trying.

Second, "How'd it go today?" sounds more like a cliché question than a genuine request for information. Cliché questions generally elicit cliché answers like "Pretty good" or "Not bad."

Finally, Midge asked the same question every day. Not only did this add to the likelihood of it being considered a cliché, but the thought of answering the same unimaginatively posed query over and over again probably bored her husband. I suggested to Midge that she read the campus newspaper and her local paper daily. Then I suggested that, after leaving her husband a little time to relax, she ask him more specific open-ended questions about interesting topics her husband was familiar with. Here's how it went:

That night, I told Mel I'd heard that the school was thinking about reinstituting the foreign language requirement for liberal arts students. I asked him what he thought about this issue. This led to our discussing whether learning a foreign language helps students better understand other people. We shared our own experiences, which led to a fun time trying to converse in rusty high school French. Finally, when we were all talked out and very happy, he gave me a little kiss and whispered, "Ah, Madame, yu arrrr magni-fique!" Now, how's that for a successful experiment?

How indeed!

The above is from Alan Garner's book, Conversationally Speaking

Conversation Ideas

Some sample questions to begin a conversation. Pick and choose.

1. What's your favorite thing to do on a rainy day?
2. If you could replay any moment in your life, what would it be?
3. What one thing would you really like to own? Why?
4. If you learned that you were going to die tomorrow, what would be the one thing you'd most regret not doing?
5. What was it like in the town where you grew up?
6. What would you like to come back as in your next life?
7. What do you think is the perfect age? Why?
8. Of all the places that you've lived, which did you like the best? Why?

9. What's your favorite holiday? What do you enjoy about it?
10. What are some of your family traditions that you particularly enjoy?
11. Tell me about the first car you ever bought.
12. Who were your idols as a kid? Have they changed?
13. Describe a memorable teacher you had.
14. Tell me about a movie/book that you've seen or read more than once.
15. What's your favorite restaurant? Why?
16. Tell me why you were named _______________.
17. What is the origin of your last name?
18. What is a place that you've visited - that you hope never to return to.
19. What's the best surprise you've ever received?
20. What's the best surprise you've ever planned for someone else?
21. Who would star as you in a movie about your life? Why that person?
22. Tell me about the best vacation you've ever taken.
23. Who is the most famous person you've met?
24. What's the most antiestablishment thing you ever did?
25. Describe a costume that you wore to a party.
26. Tell me about a political position you'd like to hold.
27. What song reminds you of an incident in your life?
28. What's the most memorable meal you've eaten?

Alan Lloyd McGinnis says in his book, The Romance Factor, "To what do you attribute the breakup of so many marriages today? Is it sexual problems, money difficulties, is it because families watch television instead of talking?

The real cause is . . . marriages die of neglect. "Not communicating is often misunderstood as not caring."

Appendix B

Classic Recipes for Classy Romance

Cooking for Two

We cooked our romantic dinners together. As the head chef in our house, I needed to be careful how many orders I gave to Jim, and what tone of voice I used, when he cooked with me. He expected to be instructed but no one likes being ordered around. Fine line there. Maybe it's the number of commands given. One or two, OK. After that it's like piling on, the football fan told me.

You might enjoy: the dining room table, your good silver, best goblets, nice placemats, flowers, candles, your favorite romantic music, a nice little wine. Look nice. I wore the clothes Jim liked. Jim wore the clothes I liked, especially the seablue shirt that matched his eyes. Later, clothing is optional. Smile, sit across from one another, don't bring up problems, flirt, remember eye contact and listening. It's time for Two-play and Three-play.

Cream Sauce

Cream Sauce for Lobster Mornay, Crab or Chicken Crepes

2 Tbsp	butter
2 Tbsp	flour
1/2 tsp	salt
speck	pepper
dash	worchestershire sauce
1 cup	milk (1 or 2% milk lowers calories)
4 Tbsp	grated parmesan cheese
2 tsp	cream sherry

Over low heat melt the butter. Stir in in salt, pepper, worchestershire and flour quickly when the butter is melted. Stir in pre-heated milk slowly but stir quickly to avoid lumps[1]. Stir often for 15 min over low heat until the sauce thickens and cooks the flour. During the last few minutes, stir in parmesan cheese and sherry.[2]

We would triple this recipe to make 5 evenings of sauce to freeze in individual portions good for Lobster Mornay or Crab or Chicken Crepes.

1 If it does get lumpy, use your hand held power mixer to smooth it out

2 You can freeze the sauce for future use, but if you do, don't put the sherry in. Instead, drink the sherry you have now, and later add sherry after the sauce has been thawed and warmed.

Lobster Mornay

Add to the cream sauce: 6-8 oz lobster meat, 2 oz grated gruyere cheese and sliced brown mushrooms, maybe thin, short strips of red bell pepper for color. Save some of the cheese to sprinkle on top.

We used about 7 or 8 oz of lobster meat. Jim would buy lobster claws and legs at Costco, frozen, and crack them himself. Hard to do. We kept band-aids handy.

Sliced mushrooms and a little onion, red pepper, sauteed first, are a delicious addition but not entirely necessary.

We served the Mornay on Trader Joe's sour dough bread toast points.

We always cooked with wine. Sometimes we even added it to the food. - paraphrasing W.C. Fields

Crepes

1	egg
1/3 cup	milk
1 tsp	melted butter
1/4 cup	flour
dash	salt
1/2 tsp	sugar
1/4 tsp	vanilla

Beat up the egg and milk and then add the rest of the ingredients.

Warm a big frying pan on a med high heat, put in 2 tsp butter or use Pam, pour in 1/2 of the crepe mixture swirling the pan to spread it thinly. Watch it and lift the edges often to see if it's browning. It browns quickly. Flip over to brown the other side. Keep the first crepe warm while cooking the second one. (The cook gets the crepe that has a hole or is not done as well.)

Line up cream sauce with lobster in the middle of the crepe and fold over the sides. Save a little cream sauce to pour over the top.

Serve with broccoli, asparagus, or whatever vegetable that gives a good presentation effect.

For Chicken or Crab Crepes, add mushrooms, chicken or crab to the sauce. The Lobster Mornay is good with the gruyere cheese. Add a sharp cheddar to the sauce with the chicken or not. Just the parmesan in the original sauce may be enough for the crab crepes.

Cheese Fondue

3/4 cup	sharp cheddar, coarsely grated
1/4 cup	blue cheese crumbles
1/2 tsp	worchestershire sauce
1/4 cup	condensed tomato soup
3 Tbsp	cream sherry

Mix all except the sherry over low heat until melted and melded.

Add sherry.

Use that old fondue pot and the long forks to dip sour dough bread cubes, apple chunks, or vege pieces.

ACKNOWLEDGEMENTS

I am so fortunate to have wonderful friends and family who have helped, encouraged and loved me while I wrote this book. Thank you from the bottom of my heart! I needed you and you were there.

Over the years the participants in Parent Effectiveness Training, Couples Communication Skills at Kaiser, Better Marriages Conferences, Marriage Enrichment classes, Happiness Groups have taught me so much.

I am so grateful to my friends in the Marriage Enrichment community for their help and encouragement: Celia and John Feret, Lynn and Roy Blom, Linda and Trev Hayes, Edna and Paul Wallace, Cathy and Muneer Waheed, Bob Griffith, Laurie Pierce, Crystal and Chris Lanier, Cindy and Lloyd Walker, Susan and Dave Sargent, Lida and Kenta Williams, Kathy and Fred Jakolat.

Thank you to my Happiness Groups and Carole and Bob Roozkowski, Christine Welch-Buck, Lynn Honkagonkas, Maria D'Avolio, Sylva Swenson.

Always there and supportive were Sandy Louthian, Nathalie Ghanthous, Jo-Ann Ash Fairbanks, Carla Gerber, Colleen Rafferty, Harriet Kawamata, Grace Schmidt, Kris Haas, Linda Krenicky, Carla Whyte.

From afar I had help from Deanna and Bob McMain, Rose and Donnel Lester, Marti and George Meister, Larry Mapp, Marilynn and Mac Dunham, Marge O'laughlin, my wonderful sons and their wives, Jim and Gerrie, Ken and Melissa, dear old friends Connie Murphy, Cass Ott, Gretchen Sherman and Carol Emshoff.

Thanks to my grandson, Kenny Strickland, for tech support.

Thomas Gordon's friendship and the book, Parent Effectiveness Training, was one of the inspirations for my life and work.

How marvelous to have my PET and Couple Communications students and weekly paragraph readers (before there was a blog) for 10 years who urged me to write a book combining all the little nudges. Thank you. Thanks so much to my genius publisher, Keith Swenson, for many months of his time and work.

And Jim Strickland who was my everything— best friend, best lover, active listener, conversation partner, Marriage Enrichment co-leader, computer fixer, jar opener, car and pool maintenence man, supporter and editor, — for 75% of my life, I am forever grateful.

BIBLIOGRAPHY

- **The Seven Principles For Making Marriage Work** – John Gottman
- **After the Fight: Using Your Disagreements to Build a Stronger Relationship** – Daniel B Wile
- **After the Honeymoon: How Conflict Can Improve Your Relationship** – Daniel B Wile
- **Fighting For Your Marriage** – Scott Stanley
- **His Needs Her Needs** – Willard Harley
- **You Just Don't Understand Me** – Deborah Tannen
- **Divorce Busting** – Michelle Weiner-Davis
- **Getting All the Love You Want** – Harville Hendrix
- **Difficult Conversations** – Douglas Stone
- **Dave Barry's Guide To Guys** – Dave Barry
- **52 Dates For You and Your Mate** – Dave and Claudia Arp
- **1001 Ways To Be Romantic** – Gregory Godek
- **The Silicon Syndrome** – Jean Hollands
- **Please Understand Me** – Kiersey and Bates
- **The 5 Love Languages** – Gary Chapman
- **Parent Effectiveness Training** – Thomas Gordon
- **Marriage For The Everyday** – Bobbye and Britton Wood
- **4 Essential Keys To Effective Communication** – Bento Leal

Index

CPSIA information can be obtained
at www.ICGtesting.com
Printed in the USA
FSHW04n1029050418
46359FS

9 780986 338762